HEALTH CARE FOR WOMEN AND GIRL CHILDREN

HEALTH CARE FOR WOMEN AND GIRL CHILDREN

S. K. Singh
Awadhesh Kr. Singh

Sponsored By
National Commission for Women
Government of India, New Delhi

In Association with
PANDIT GOVIND BALLABH PANT INSTITUTE OF STUDIES
IN RURAL DEVELOPMENT, LUCKNOW

SERIALS PUBLICATIONS
NEW DELHI

First Published - 2009

ISBN: 978-81-8387-189-1

Published by

SERIALS PUBLICATIONS
4830/24, Prahlad Street, Ansari Road
Darya Ganj, New Delhi-110002 (India)
Phone : 23245225. Fax : 91-11-23272135
E-mail: serials@satyam.net.in

CONTENTS

PREFACE AND ACKNOWLEDGEMENT

It is well recognized that improvement in the health status of population is both an important means of increasing productivity and economic growth as well as an end in itself. The importance of improvements in health is also acknowledged in the Millennium Development Goals of the UNDP, which calls for a dramatic reduction in poverty and improvements in health, especially of the poor. In India, with its vast majority of poor population, ensuring the good health of the people is a challenging task.

India is expecting to be world's most populated country by 2050 leaving aside China. It is a country with limited resources to feed unlimited population. Its decadal growth of population is more than the population of Brazil. If such trends continue then there will be population explosion. Ironically India was the first country to launch family planning programmes in 1952 and then kept on changing strategies in relation to international conferences like that of Mexico, Cairo, Beijing etc. with limited success. The fact remains that Government alone cannot successfully restrict family size avail health services and bring development. There is a need of collaboration with voluntary agencies, grass root level leaders and the masses in this regard.

Against this backdrop, present study has been carried out to examine the health status of women and children in the states of Uttar Pradesh and Uttaranchal. It presents detailed account of health care services for women and children in the two states. The study has been planned in 7 chapters. Chapter 1st is introductory one which gives brief account of rational, objectives and research methodology. Chapter 2nd is concerned with health care services for women and children in India. An interstate analysis of data pertaining to health care services has been given in the chapter in order to understand the dynamics of health status of women and children. Chapter 3rd is related to reproductive health status of married adolescent girls. It gives an account of socio-economic status of adolescent girls, reproductive and sexual health needs and their problems related with their reproductive health. Chapter 4th provides background of the respondents and their living conditions. Chapter 5th gives detailed account of health seeking behaviour, health status and access and quality of health care services. Chapter 6th is concerned with view perception of officials and non-officials. Chapter 7th is concluding one which provides the basis for main findings, observations and policy recommendations.

Disabled are most marginalized. The problem of disability in India has posed serious challenges and constraints for rehabilitation of physically and mentally challenged persons. Modernization, liberalisation and globalization have related resulted in increased rate of disability. More than 10 per cent of the country's population is comprising of Physically and mentally challenged persons. About 40 per cent of disabled are children. This is a serious concern for policy makers child thus rehabilitation is imperative.

The study has been the outcome of cooperation, support, encouragement, and vigour extended by several people from time to time. The authors are grateful to the concerned officials of the National Commission for Women, Ministry of Women and Child Development, Govt. of India for entrusting the study to the Institute and extending financial support. Without their support, the study could have not been possible.

We are thankful to the staff and officials of Directorate of Health and Family Welfare, Government of Uttar Pradesh and Uttaranchal for their cooperation and assistance. Dr. R.V.P. Singh, Planning Commission, Government of India, deserves special mention for extending support and cooperation for early access to resource literature. The research team traveled in the tough terrain and in remote areas in difficult situations and completed the field work. They deserve a special mention for their untiring efforts. We also thank Sourabth Pandey in assisting us in the drafting state. Finally, we are thankful to M/s Serial Publications to have taken up the responsibility of publication.

We are thankful to the Ministry Social Justice & Empowerment, New Delhi for instructing the Study or social rehabilitations of disabled children. The concerned officials of rehabilitation centres and NGO, Non-extended are kind of cooperation and assistance in smooth conduct of the study.

The rehabilitation centres of Allahabad, Kanpur, Varanasi were selected for the study and the concerned officials assisted the research team for field survey. We are thankful to the children of these centres who also assisted research team for their interview.

We are indebted to Dr. S.P. Pandey, Director of the Institute in extending full cooperation during completion of the study.

S. K. Singh &
A. K. Singh

1

INTRODUCTION

India is expecting to be world's most populated country by 2050 leaving aside China. India is a country with limited resources to feed unlimited population. The decadal growth of population is more than the population of Brazil. If such trends continue then there will be population explosion. Ironically, India was the first country to launch family planning programmes in 1952 and then kept on changing its strategies in relation to international conferences like that of Mexico, Cairo, Beijing etc. with limited success. The fact remains that Government alone cannot successfully restrict family size, avail health services and bring development. There is urgent need of collaboration with voluntary agencies, grass root level leaders and the masses.

The present programme structure of the Family Welfare Department of the Ministry of Health and Family Welfare, Government of India, New Delhi, is complex and has been built up overtime. New projects and programmes have been added to the original core of family planning programmes for example MCH, CSSM, and RCH etc. In the 7th Plan (1984–89) Maternal and Child Health (MCH) component was added with focus on the health needs of women in reproductive age group and children under five in addition to providing contraceptives and spacing services to the married couples. Similarly, the Child

Survival and Safe Motherhood (CSSM) Programme was launched in 1992 with the assistance from the World Bank and UNICEF to strengthen the maternal and child health component of National Family Welfare Programme. The CSSM included components like management of acute respiratory track infections, diarrhea care and emergency obstetric services. It was first serious attempt at integrating issues pertaining to morbidity, mortality and quality of life of pregnant mothers and infants. International Conference on Population and Development, 1994 at Cairo recommended that the participating countries should implement unified programmed for RCH. The concept of RCH was to provide the beneficiaries need based, client centered, demand driven high quality and integrated health services handling to population stabilization. The RCH package of India is consisting of (i) prevention and management of unwanted fertility, (ii) management of pregnancy and child birth; (iii) prevention and management of RTI's and STD's; (iv) child survival through immunization, diarrhea and acute respiratory illness control and care to newborn etc. As National Population Policy, 2000 has assigned important role to community based organizations (Panchayats, NGOs, Youth Clubs, SHGs) for implementation, monitoring and management of the RCH programmes at the grass root level, Village self-help groups are to be utilized to organize and provide basic services for RCH combined with the ongoing Integrated Child Development Scheme. Integrated and coordinated service delivery package for basic health care, family planning and maternal child health related services will be provided at village level by the community and for the community. The NGOs were also encouraged to participate in the operation of RCH programmes.

In 1943, the Government of India appointed the historical Bhore Committee to survey the health situation in the country and make recommendations for the future. Remarkably influenced by the considerations of the Beveridge Committee in England, which gave birth to the National Health Service in the country, the Bhore Committee made far reaching recommendations guided by two overriding principles. First, the position of health care services was the responsibility of the state, second, comprehensive health care should be available to people irrespective of their ability to pay. The blueprint for the development of health services that was outlined, both in the short–term and long–term, emphasized preventive services, focusing on rural areas and linking health with overall development. In the First Plan, more than half of the expenditure was allocated for development of hospitals and dispensaries and 40 per cent of the total provision was allocated for medical education and training. Primary health centres were to be developed as part of the Community Development Programme. The First Plan gave birth to the launch of what are called multipurpose, vertical programmes for the control of malaria, small pox, filaria, leprosy, cholera and venereal diseases. India was the first country in the world to launch a family planning programme during this period. While recognizing the importance of maternal and child health, this was to form an integral component of the general health services. In the Second Plan, encouraged by international agencies, the control programmes was converted into the National Malaria Eradication Programme. It was envisaged that malaria would be eradicated by 1966. The operational strategy for the family planning programme over the first two plan periods, inspired by international agencies, was the clinical approach. The Third Plan witnessed the coming to the fore recommendations of the Health Survey and Planning Committee, known in popular parlance as the Mudaliar Committee. The committee noted that the primary health care system that had evolved so very haltingly, bear no resemblance to that visualized by the Bhore Committee. The committee recommended the up-gradation of existing services. In 1962, National Tuberculosis Programme was launched following a series of small pox eradication programme. This finally started paying dividends although when India finally eradicated small pox in 1975, it had not only poured in much more resources than had been anticipated. In the Fourth Plan, the pace of the family planning programme was substantially accelerated; family welfare centres for vasectomy were supplemented by more than 1000 mobile service units. In 1972–73, sterilization reached a peak of 3.1 million. Two thirds of these performed in camps. The World Bank and the Population Council endorsed developmentalist perspective of the country.

The echoes of such shifts reverberated in India as the Fifth Plan codified this changed perspective. It noted that the primary objective is to provide minimum public health facilities integrated with family planning and nutrition for vulnerable groups. The year 1975 enters the annals of the history of public health in India for two reasons. First in this year, India finally was declared small pox free. Second, the year witnessed the declaration of emergency which facilitated the passage of the draconian National Population Policy of April 1976 which called for a direct assault on the population problem. In 1977, the government announced the implementation of scheme for strengthening rural health care services. In this year, Community Health Volunteers Scheme was inaugurated as a step towards repositioning people's hands on a war footing. In 1980, 'Health for All', An Alternative Strategy was adopted. This strategy *routed* in the community, provided adequate, efficient and equitable referral services, integrated and promoted preventive and curative aspects and combined the valuable elements in our culture and tradition with the best elements of the Western System. The Sixth Plan adopted a long-term demographical goal of reducing the net reproduction rate of one by all the states of the country by 2001. Towards this end, it recognized the need for poverty eradication, improvements in infant and child survival and nutrition. Thus, in the plan period, there was an increasing emphasis on the sterilization of women, often at laparoscopic camps. Health programmes that were included in the 20 Point Programme, viz., tuberculosis, leprosy, and UIP were now assigned targets to be achieved while the CHV scheme was unceremoniously buried. The Seventh Plan noted the inability to meet the targets set out both for rural infrastructure development and control of communicable diseases in the Sixth Plan, it sets no contradiction in commending the development of specialties and super specialties to grapple with the major health problem of non-communicable diseases. During this period natural AIDS control programme commenced with a soft loan of US$ 84 million from World Bank and technical assistance from WHO.

A separate organization, the NACO, was consequently set up. The Eighth Plan document again notes the depressingly familiar inability to meet the goals of the previous plan in control of communicable diseases, in achieving the family planning goals. During this period, AIDS control began to assume increasing importance, not so much because it was assessed as a major public health problem epidemiologically, but because funds began flowing from international agencies. The Ninth Plan stated that reduction in the population growth rate has been recognized as one of the priority objectives during the Plan period. The priorities in the Plan were started to be to meet the felt needs for contraception, and to reduce the infant and maternal morbidity and mortality so that there was a reduction in the desired level of fertility. During this period, two important policy documents were announced, first the National Population Policy, significantly announced earlier, the second, the National Health Policy.

National Population Policy 2000 also envisages improving the quality of lives that people lead through providing opportunities and choices to become productive assets in the society. India's population as projected to be one billion, about sixteen per cent of the world's population, is continue to increase and likely to overtake China in 2045. Thus national socio-demographic goals for 2010 include mainly addressing the unmet needs for basic reproductive and child health services, and infrastructure; reducing infant and maternal mortality rates; achieving universal immunization of children against all vaccine preventable diseases; promoting delayed marriage for girls; achieving 80% institutional deliveries and 100% deliveries by trained persons; achieving universal access to information, counseling and services for fertility regulation and contraception; achieving 100% registration of births, deaths, marriages, pregnancies; reducing the vulnerability of HIV/AIDS and other communicable diseases etc.

International consensus has emerged to reduce indices/ deaths arising out of communicable and preventable diseases, as indicated by three of the eight Millennium Development Goals. Keeping 1990s as the benchmark, the three goals and targets that have to be achieved by 2015 are (i) to reduce under five (infant/child) mortality by two thirds, (ii) to reduce maternal mortality rate by three fourths; and (iii) to combat human immunodeficiency virus/acquired immune deficiency syndrome (HIV/AIDS), malaria, tuberculosis (TB) and other diseases by not only halting their rising incidences but also by reversing their spread. India Vision 2020 envisages increasing access to health care for women and children, eliminating childhood deaths from diarrhea by 2010, effective targeting of undernourished children, restructuring malaria workforce to reduce incidence by 50 per cent and improving *diagnosis* and *treatment of TB*. It also seeks to address the state of *under equipped, under staffed* and *under financed* health care infrastructure and suggests increasing public spending from 0.8 per cent to 3.4 per cent of gross domestic product.

Effective public health measures need to address issues of food, hygiene, availability of clean air and water and proper sanitation. Designing of public policy should factor in local specifications, with decentralization and devolution of power, the local bodies will have a greater role. Addressing state, district or block specific public policy does not mean doing away with the role of the Central Government. It requires the Centre to be more proactive in addressing inequalities across states and to ensure appropriate regulatory and monitoring mechanisms. The presence of NGOs and CBOs is lower in poorer regions. There is need to increase the number of care providers and create suitable working conditions to ensure their availability in remote areas.

The Ministry of Health & Family Welfare (MOHFW), Government of India is implementing a Reproductive Child Health (RCH) Programme in the country. For this purpose, it is absolutely essential to obtain knowledge of the existing situation at different levels of health facilities in the country.

A facility survey at district level will help in assessing the availability of trained staff, equipment and supplies and their utilization at Primary Health Centres (PHCs), Community Health Centres (CHCs), First Referral Units (FRUs) and District Hospitals.

It is well recognized that improvement in the health status of population is both an important means of increasing productivity and economic growth as well as an end in itself. It is also acknowledged in the Millennium Development Goals of the UNDP, which calls for a dramatic reduction in poverty and improvements in health, especially of the poor. In India, with its vast majority of poor population, ensuring the good health of the people is a challenging task. To deal with this enormous challenge, the Government of India formulated the National Health Policy, 1983, which set some health-related targets to be achieved by 1985, 1990 and 2000. However, barring a few exceptions such as life expectancy, polio immunization, and crude death rate, these targets remained unachieved. It is clear that those health systems that direct their resources and energies towards the health needs of the poor have a better overall health status. This is a logical association, since the poor carry the larger burden of disease. But the facts make a mockery of such logic as they establish the raw deal the poor are getting from the public health care system. A recent study by the Economic Research reveals that the richest 20 per cent enjoy three times the share of public subsidy for health compound with the poorest quintile. The poorest 20 per cent of Indians have more than double the mortality rates, fertility rates and under-nutrition levels of the richest 20 per cent. The poor suffer disproportionately more from pre-transition diseases such as malaria, and T.B. on an average, they spend 12 per cent of their incomes on health care, as opposed to only 2 per cent spend by the rich. Treatment or hospitalization for chronic illness often means the liquidation of meagre assets, even permanent indebtedness. One episode of hospitalization is enough to wipe out all the assets of the family. It is no wonder then that the number of the poor who did not seek treatment because of financial reasons increased from 15 per cent to 24 per cent in rural areas and doubled from 10 per cent to 21 per cent in urban areas in the 1986-96 decade.

The obvious and most important reason is that for a state that promises universal health care through the public health system, India has one of the lowest health budgets in the world. The state's role in health has fallen well short of its declared intentions. It failed to provide health care to the majority of the population through the public sector. In the context of a public health system that does not deliver services to those who need them, the private sector has to be the main provider of curative health care. Thus, deprivation and vulnerability make the poor ill more easily, and illness makes them ever poorer and marginalized.

Children below 5 and women in the reproductive age group (15-44 years) constitute 36.2 per cent of the Indian population. In terms of survival and well being, they also make up the most vulnerable group in society. Efforts to improve their survival rates and health status have a long history in India. Successive Five Year Plan documents have enunciated a strong MCH component, but from the Third Five Year Plan period, the overriding focus has been population control. Even after the transition of the programme from family planning to family welfare, and the launching of the expanded programme of Immunization in 1979, the Universal Immunization Programme in 1985, and the Child Survival and Safe Motherhood Programme in 1990, MCH Services have frequently been crowded out by family planning. Significantly, family planning services can reduce pregnancies, and the majority of their complications and child birth can be prevented/treated by comprehensive antenatal care, which would effectively screen and treat high risk cases and ensure that such deliveries take place in adequately equipped health institutions. Safe abortion services would also reduce maternal mortality. However, 15-20 per cent of pregnant women develop complications during child-birth most of which cannot be predicted.

Reproductive health of women in India has been usually seen related to their reproductive roles as mothers. Reproductive health care has been around ensuring safe child-birth and contraception. The RCH Programme, which was introduced in 1997 has the following main features:

(i) Prevention and management of unwanted pregnancy through education and counseling, contraceptive services and safe abortion services upto 20 weeks of pregnancy.

(ii) Maternal care including treatment of malaria, tuberculosis, RTI's and sexually transmitted diseases during the antenatal period in addition to interventions already included under the child survival and safe motherhood programme.

(iii) Child survival services for new born and infants including better neonatal care, immunization, promotion of breast-feeding, ORT for diarrhoeal diseases, detection and referral of premature babies, low birth weight babies, severe dehydration, acute respiratory infections etc. and

(iv) Prevention and management of RTI's and sexually transmitted diseases, HIV and AIDS through education, counseling and also detection and treatment.

The programme aims to improve quality and coverage of health care to women, children and adolescents, so that their felt needs for health care are fully met. Interestingly, the sexual and reproductive health situation and choices of married adolescent girls differ from adult women. There is a need to raise awareness among parents/teachers and community leaders and also to hold government accountable for enforcing the legal age of marriage. It is said that early marriage of girl children, poor health and nutrition of pregnant and lactating mothers and poor status of vaccination and immunization of girl children are the cause of high mortality rates among infants and children. Again, poor nutritional status of infants and girl children is also causing high mortality rates.

The extent of access to and utilization of health care varied substantially between states, districts and different segments of society; this to a large extent, is responsible for substantially differences between states in health indices of the population.

During the 1990s, the mortality rates reached a plateau and the country entered an era of dual disease burden. Communicable diseases have become more difficult to combat because of development of insecticide resistant strains of vectors, antibiotics resistant strains of bacteria and emergence of HIV infection for which there is no therapy. Longevity and changing life style have resulted in the increasing prevalence of non-communicable diseases. Under nutrition, micro nutrient deficiencies and associated health problems coexist with obesity and non-communicable diseases. The existing health system suffers from inequitable distribution of institutions and manpower. Even though the country produces over 17,000 doctors in modern system of medicine and similar number of ISM&H practitioners and paraprofessionals, there are huge gaps in critical manpower in institutions providing primary health care, especially in the remote rural and tribal areas where health needs are the greatest.

As the country undergoes demographic and epidemiological transition, it is likely that larger investments in health will be needed even to maintain the current health status because tackling resistant infections and non-communicable diseases will inevitably lead to escalating health care costs. Last two decades have witnessed explosive expansion in expensive health care related technologies and broadening diagnostic and therapeutic avenues. Increasing awareness and rising expectations to access these have widened the gap between what is possible and what is affordable for the individual or the country. Policy makers and programme managers realise that in order to address the increasingly complex situation regarding access to good quality care at affordable costs, it is essential to build up an integrated health system with appropriate screening, regulating access at different levels and referral linkages. However, both health care providers and health care seekers still feel more comfortable with the one-to-one relationship then with the health system approach.

Another problem is the popular perception that curative and preventive care compete for available resources, with the former getting preference in funding. Efforts to convince the public that preventive and curative care are both part of the entire spectrum of health care ranging from health promotion, specific protection, early diagnosis and prompt treatment, disability limitation and rehabilitation and that to improve the health status of the population both are equally essential have not been very successful. Traditionally, health service (both government and private) was perceived as a social responsibility albeit a paid one. Growing commercialization of health care and medical education over the last two decades has eroded this commitment, adversely affecting the quality of care, trust and the rapport between health care seekers and providers.

Faced with the problems of sub-optimally functioning health care system and providing adequate investment for improving health, Ninth Plan emphasized the need for:

- Reviewing the changing health scenario and assess response of the public, voluntary and private sector health care providers as well as the population themselves to the changing situation.
- Reorganizing health systems so that they become efficient and effective.
- Introducing health system reforms which ensure access to public health programmes free of cost to all and enable the population to obtain essential health care at affordable cost.

The Health Care System Consists of:

- Primary, secondary and tertiary care institutions, manned by medical and paramedical personnel;
- Medical colleges and para-professional training institutions to train the needed manpower and give the required academic input;
- Programme managers managing ongoing programmes at central, state and district levels; and
- Health management information system consisting of a two-way system of data collection, collation, analysis and response.

Major initiatives of Government include:

- Reorganization and restructuring of the existing government health care system including the ISM&H infrastructure at the primary, secondary and tertiary care levels with appropriate referral linkages. These institutions will have the responsibility of taking care of all the health problems (communicable, non-communicable diseases) and deliver Reproductive and Child Health (RCH) services for people residing in a well-defined geographic urban and rural area;
- Development of appropriate two-way referral systems utilizing Information Technology (IT) tools to improve communication, consultation and referral right from primary care to tertiary care level;
- Building up an efficient and effective logistics system for the supply of drugs, vaccines and consumables based on need and utilisation;
- Horizontal integration of all aspects of the current vertical programmes including supplies, Monitoring, Information Education Communication and Motivation (IECM), Training, Administrative Arrangements and Implementation so that they are integral components of health care; there will be progressive convergence of funding, implementation and monitoring of all health and family welfare programmes under a single field of administration beginning at and below district level;
- Mainstreaming ISM&H practitioners, so that in addition to practicing their system of care, they can help in improving the coverage of the National Disease Control Programmes and Family Welfare Programme;
- Increasing the involvement of voluntary and private organizations, self-help groups and social marketing organisation in improving access to health care;
- Improving the efficiency of the existing health care system in the government, private and voluntary sectors and building up appropriate linkages between them;

- Building up tele-linkages between villages, Subcentre, PHC, FRU, district and tertiary care centres; linking tertiary care institutions especially in the remote areas (*e.g.* north-eastern states) with major super-specialty institutions for other regions so that patients could benefit from tele-consultations;
- Increasing use of Information Technology for health management. All sub-sectors dealing with the generation, transmission and utilisation of demographic and epidemiological data such as bio-informatics, bio-statistics, HMIS and the Decision Support Systems (DSS) will be used in health planning and management building up a fully functional, accurate Health Management Information System (HMIS) utilising currently available IT tools; this real time communication link will send data on births, deaths, diseases, request for drugs, diagnostics and equipment and status of ongoing programmes through service channels within existing infrastructure and manpower and funding; it will also facilitate decentralized district based planning, implementation and monitoring;
- Building up an effective system of disease surveillance and response at the district, state and national level as a part of existing health services; and
- Improving inter-sectoral coordination.

The Integrated Reproductive and Child Health Programme (1996) was also landed. The features of the programmes are:

- Prevention and management of unwanted pregnancy through education and counseling, contraceptive and safe abortion services upto 20 weeks of pregnancy;
- Maternal care including treatment of malaria, tuberculosis, RTIs and sexually transmitted diseases during the antenatal period in addition to interventions already included under the Child Survival and Safe Motherhood Programme;
- Child survival services for new born and infants including better neo-natal care, immunization, promotion of breast-

feeding. ORT for diarrhoeal diseases, detection and referrals of premature babies, low birth weight babies, severe dehydration, Acute Respiratory Infections (ARI) etc; and

- Prevention and management of RTIs and sexually transmitted diseases, HIV and AIDS through education, counseling and also detection and treatment.

  Reproductive and Child Health Programme was launched in October 1997,which aims to improve quality and coverage of health care to women, children and adolescents, so that their felt needs for health care are fully met. In addition efforts will be made to improve the participation of men in the planned-parenthood movement. Prevention and control of Sexually Transmitted Disease (STD)/Reproductive Tract Infection (RTI) including emerging problem of HIV/AIDS will also receive due attention.

The components of Reproductive Health Care are:

- Effective maternal care to ensure safe motherhood;
- Increased access to contraceptive care to prevent unwanted pregnancies;
- Legal abortion facilities for safe management of unwanted pregnancies;
- Effective nutritional services to vulnerable groups;
- Prevention and treatment of RTI/STD;
- Reproductive health services for adolescents;
- Prevention and treatment of gynecological problems including infertility, menstrual disorders and prolapsed uterus;
- Screening and treatment of cancers, especially that of uterine cervix and breast;
- Increased male participation.
- It envisaged that while providing the package of services efforts would be made to improve the quality of services;
- Services made more responsive to users' needs;

- Ensure that health workers and health care providers have the necessary skills;
- Ensure supplies needed for delivery of service, and
- Strong and effective referral system to manage all the risk cases.

REVIEW OF LITERATURE

A number of studies have been conducted dealing with concepts of disease and healing, health practices, demographic change, nutritional status, health seeking behaviour, etc. Much of the development of medical anthropology has occurred since World War II. The study of human confrontations with disease and illness and of the adaptive arrangements (that is, medicines and medical systems) made by human groups for dealing with these has come to be known as medical Anthropology (Landy, 1977). By the early 1960s the term Medical Anthropology had come to be used increasingly by Anthropologists working in and around problems in health and disease in human societies. The term was used by many scholars (Caudill, 1953), (Polgar, 1962), (Scotch, 1963), (Hughes, 1968), (Fabrega, 1972), (Lieban, 1973), (Foster and Anderson, 1978).

Medical Anthropology encompasses the study of medical phenomenon as they are influenced by social and cultural features and social and cultural phenomena as they are illuminated by their medical aspects (Lieban, 1973). Medical Anthropology includes interests and contributions from all the branches of Anthropology. Without this broad, bio-cultural approach, the use of the ecological framework, already so promising in other sub-disciplines of Anthropology which has made an initial impact in the medical Anthropological area, will not be utilized. Compared to most other disciplines, the hallmark of Anthropology, medical Anthropology included, is the so-called holistic approach. The medical Anthropologists collect a great deal of data about economic features, social relationships, cultural belief systems, political processes, and other aspects of a community, even if the research is focused on a specific health question. Medical Anthropology deals with people's point of view in medicine. There are different schools of thought in medical Anthropology. These are culture trait approach (Clement, 1932); functional approach (Ackernecht, 1958; Mead, 1953, Foster, 1979); (Paul, 1955); symbolic approach (Turner, 1964); semantic approach (Good, 1977; Fabrega, 1978; Kleinmann and Sung, 1979). Medical Anthropology is concerned with the bio-cultural understanding of man and his works in relation to health and medicine (Alland, 1966; Roney, 1959, 1963; Scotch, 1963). While this bio-cultural orientation is basic to the whole field of Anthropology, medical Anthropology as a subspecialty or as a "synthetic discipline" with multidisciplinary orientations may involve medical scientists, anthropologists, biologists, and sociologists (Roney, 1959, 1963). It has been observed that medical Anthropology is the holistic study of health, illness and related misfortunes, as these are culturally perceived, labeled, classified, experienced and communicated on one hand and socially constructed roles, statuses and institutional networks which are believed to help in the health enhancing process, on the other, with a view to identify cross-cultural similarities and variations in the patterning of such behaviour. Medical Anthropology, therefore, is a bio-cultural discipline concerned with both biological and socio-cultural aspects of human behaviour, particularly with the ways in which the two interact and have interacted throughout human history to influence the conceptions of health and treatments and therapies of disease (Foster and Anderson, 1978).

Renowned Anthropologists namely Rieves (1924) and Clements (1932) have made significant contributions in the field of concept of health and disease. Clements had tried to trace the worldwide distribution of five basic concepts of disease, viz. sorcery, and breach of taboo, object intrusion, spirit intrusion and soul loss. A number of other valuable studies, which appeared in the 1930's also deserve mention. These include field's study of the Ga People (1973) and Spencer's study of disease, religion and society in the Fiji Islands (1941). In the Indian cultural setting, numerous studies on the etiology, diagnosis and therapy of diseases have been carried out in different communities by Gould (1957), Khare (1963), Hasan (1967), Madan (1969), Rizvi (1991), Bhat (1986) and Das (1986) etc.

National Family Health Survey, 1998-99 has also highlighted the poor health status of women in India. Total fertility rate was reported 3.06 among Scheduled Castes as compared to 2.85 in total population. Infant and child mortality rates have been recorded higher in tribal population as compared to non-tribal population. Childhood vaccination has been found lower in tribal population as compared to non-tribal population. The nutritional status of tribal women has also been found to be lower since they are more anemic and take poor nutritional diet. More than 64.9 per cent tribal women were reported to be anemic while this rate in general population has been found just 51.8 per cent. About 80 per cent child population from Scheduled Tribes has been found anemic while this rate is 74.3 per cent in general population. Only 10 per cent tribal women are getting antenatal care at home while 43.1 per cent women do not get any antenatal checkup. This percentage is higher than the general population. 70.4 per cent deliveries are done at home in the tribal population.

Reddy and Reddy (2002) discussed the role of folk medicine among the tribal people of Nallamala region of Andhra Pradesh. They said that diseases like jaundice, stomach pain, dysentery, headache, cough, fevers during rainy season, rheumatism, sprain bore features and pains in any region ascribed to natural causes and they are cured only by administering herbal medicine. Reddy, *et.al.* (2002) studied that health and nutritional programme among the Yerukalas of Prakasam district of Andhra Pradesh has impacted tribals to a great extent. Singh has studied in detail the population structure and biological micro-differentiation among Bhoxas of U.P. (1993) and also analysed the emerging trends of mortality among them (2003).

Maharatna has investigated in to a very interesting aspect of women work participation, their contribution to the pool of family income and the impact of the free participation on the pressure of work, workload and available leisure to the females. It is reported that the participation is in the spirit of work sharing as well as in the spirit of independent entrepreneurship. In mountainous regions, the workload is the result of the topographical and climatic disadvantage coupled by the absence of any worth, while technology to reduce the drudgery of work. The total workload is too great for women and ultimate available leisure to women in hills of Uttar Pradesh is too short. The males seem to shift the work on the female even if it is avoidable. Author observes that the Garhwal women have relatively greater willingness and access to educational amenities and in fact the literacy rates suggest this. But this does not seem to save them from the excessive workload and drudgery of routine. The paper gives the impression that education of females is likely to affect fertility in the longer perspective.

A.K. Kapoor in his scholastic paper on 'Ecology, Demographic Profiles & Socio-economic Development of Tribes in Central Himalaya' investigates the developmental problems and demographic profiles of sub-groups of Bhotia tribe in 20 habitations of Central Himalaya. Beside the demographic data which the author has meticulously complied and processed, he presents interesting facts on the three successive settlements in migration process which Bhotias keep for the varying seasons. The paper assesses the impact of Sino-Indian border conflict on the infrastructural growth as well as development programmes for areas enclosing Bhotia settlements.

Kapoor concludes that development has ignored population control and fertility regulation so also the environment sustainability as objectives. The rapidity of urbanization and inter-region disparities and ecological disaster are the results of faulty strategies, and careless implementation of development projects. Author feels that the population settled in UP Hills has to suffer for obvious reasons of poor resource base, paucity of arable land, absence of irrigation and non-availability of investment fund coupled with unprecedented population growth and fall in mortality. Encroachments in forests and disappearance of village common grass-lands, overlapping of trees for foliage and too many cattle have deteriorated the overall availabilities. The region abounds in extreme disparities at social and economic counts. This case study covers Johari, Rang, Marcha, Tochla and Jad wings of Bhotia tribe. The area under study is hilly tracts of Garhwal and Kumaun divisions of Uttar Pradesh. Bhotia tribe has Mongoloid origin ethnically. They are more alike Kumaunese and Garhwalis than the Tibetan counterparts. They have their own unique cultural traits. Snow clad peaks, glaciers, streams, rugged mountains, forests and shrubs around; make the surroundings of Bhotia habitations. In Chaudans, Johar and Niti valleys the Bhotia population settles in agricultural occupation. In other habitations Bhotia households are more or less migratory. The habitations are between 3500 to 14000 feet elevation. Bhotias are a successful business tribe but they have lost their business-clientele due to elimination of Indo-Tibetan trade. Now this trade, though reopened, has only a nominal existence.

Kapoor reports extremely varying sex ratio, at birth, among the subgroups of Bhotias. In some groups, females are few while among others their number is disproportionately greater. Mean age at marriage for females is 18-19 years while mean age at the first pregnancy is 20 years. These averages are no way comparable with the data reported for UP plains. Average fertility is any way less among the Bhotias as compared to their non-tribe counterparts. The fertility range is 4.57 to 6.30 per married female. GFR is ranging between 162.4 and 175.2 among subgroups. Crude death rate ranges between 12.27 and 16.11. This shows the difference in CDR in plains of UP and the Bhotia tribe. It can probably be explained as impact of climate and difficult living conditions among Bhotias. After closure of trade, Bhotias have suffered loss of occupation and have tried to concentrate on farming and animal husbandry. The flocks of sheep and Yak in higher elevation have become redundant. Shortage of wool as raw material for their domestic craft has rendered women folk without work and deprived them from traditional crafts-based incomes. The land of Bhotia tribes which was being tolled by tenants in the period of trade has now been transferred to them permanently by Zamindari abolition. It is only after China-India conflict that government started attending to their needs and basic amenities. The exposure of this tribe to towns of wider Indian plains and official reservations for tribes in government jobs, coupled by an easy access to education at low cost have benefited Bhotia youth tremendously. The rural youth, however, have lost industrious habits and found easy money making methods of illicit distillation in large measure. They hardly use any fertilizers and insecticides in farming but use manure adequately. Their poor habitat, niggardly nature and precarious tract do not permit much of agricultural future. Educated youth finding government jobs lucrative and better than trade, industry and farming pushed up out-migration. Since the tribe, had by far, better economic background and business acumen, the Bhotia boys have fast adapted to higher education. The other tribes like Raji and Jaunsaries are far behind the Bhotias today.

Invariably, data on absorption and still birth are under reported. One of the reasons could be their inability to share such sensitive information with the field workers who often stay there for a short period. And since most of them are non-clinicians, it becomes difficult to persuade the tribal people regarding the rationale of seeking such information. It takes time before people are convinced about the purpose of such information.

A general indicator of the health of girls and women is their life expectancy. The expectation of life is the average number of years remaining to be lived by those surviving. The expectation of life at birth is the life table function most frequently used as an index of the level of mortality. It also represents a summarization of the whole series of mortality rates for all ages combined as weighted by the life table stationary population.

Rao *et. al.* (1954) has dealt with the problem of health and disease in Nainital. The authors observed that folkways centered around effect of image for cure of disease by shutting and preventing recourse to modern medicine. They also point out that indigenous medicines have the advantages in the context of folkways, the force of tradition, the conformation of mythology and legend, the prestige of strong personalities who act as functionaries, etc. They are interwoven with the common artifacts and techniques of daily existence and are easily available and inexpensive.

Carastairs (1955) in his study pointed out that the difference between the points of view of the physicians and the village folk with regard to the theory of etiology, techniques of curing and conceptions of roles of the physicians, resulted in misunderstanding between himself, a physician and his client.

Marriott (1955) conducted study on village Kishan Garhi in Aligarh district of Uttar Pradesh. This study tries to explore the problems of introducing western medicine in Indian village community. He has shown how the contracts and conflicts between the roles assumed by the indigenous and western medicinal practitioners resulted in obstacles to the acceptability of western medicine.

Hasan (1967) distinguishes between two types of social and cultural factors that affect the health of any community; (a) factors that directly affect the health of the community because certain customs, practices, beliefs, values and religious taboos etc. create an environment that helps in the spread or control of certain disease and (b) factors that indirectly affect the health of the community as they are related to the problem of medical care to the sick and the invalid. A physician, who does not try to understand that cultural and intellectual level of the people and does not develop respect for cultural differences, proves to be a less successful. If scientific medicine is to be carried to rural areas, it is necessary for medical practitioners and public health workers to acquire adequate knowledge of the general concept of culture and social organisation of that community.

Singh et. al. (1986) pointed out that any treatment involves two individuals, the healer and the patient; one requires the cooperation of both of them. Unfortunately, when a system of medicine has its roots in alien culture, there is conflict between different cultural values resulting in the rejection of the alien system by the recipient. The best way to overcome this problem is to understand the indigenous medical beliefs and practices and allow western medicine to find its place by following the cultural noı ms of the society in which it operates.

Jaggi (1973) has discussed how the nature of treatment varies with the type of cause identified. For example, religious rites occupy a prominent place in the treatment of diseases, which are associated with supernatural causes to the exclusion of other factors.

Bannerji (1982) discussed an unequal access to the health services between the social classes, the privileged and underprivileged and between rural and urban areas in the country. He pointed out that the frequent realization to take action to meet the health services need of the poor and to entrust "Peoples health in People's hand" indicates conceptual watershed to some significance in health services development in the country as this showed subordination of medical technology to the needs of the health.

Mitras *et. al.* (1998) have examined the various environments, socio-economic and cultural factors whose interplay determines the health of pregnant and nursing mothers in 'Bhumiheen camp', a slum in Govindpuri, South Delhi. They have tried to understand the health problems and practices of slum women and the role of socio-economic and physical environment in influencing them. They have found that the most direct effects of poor health and nutrition among females in countries like India are high mortality rates among young children and women of child-bearing age and high morbidity rates throughout the life cycle. The effects of pervasive ill health extend beyond the women. Women's health and nutritional status is bound up with social, cultural and economic factors that influence all aspects of their lives, and it has consequences not only for the women themselves but also for the well-being of the family and functioning of households. For improving the health status of poor women, greater opportunities of schooling and employment as well as some changes in health system are needed, to increase the demand for health services and women's ability to use them. They have found that a perceived relation between poor surroundings and sickness exists among slum women.

It has been observed that Health and treatment reflects the social solidarity of a community. In a tribal community, for example, illness and the consequent treatment is not always an individual or a familial affair, but the decision about the nature of treatment is taken at the community level. In the rural areas, in case of some specific diseases, not only the diseased person or his/her family, but also the total village community is affected. All the other families in the village are expected to observe certain taboos or norms and food habits. The non-observance of such practices often calls for action by the village council. One cannot deny the impact of this psychological support in the context of treatment and cure. In some societies, illness may be an individual affair, and the patient may be looked after by the administration (state), while in tribal societies it is a familial or sometimes community affair where necessary action and care is taken by the community as a whole.

Maternal and child-care is an important aspect of health seeking behaviour. Maternal malnutrition leads to premature deliveries, low birth weight babies and pregnancy wastages. Data on this aspect is fragmentary on the tribal population groups of India. Nevertheless, the trends that are coming up are alarming. In one of the study on Bhotia, Kapoor and Prasad (1982) have observed that in the event of delayed conception of married women, the deities like Nanda Devi, Nabling and Kalika are propitiated by taking on earthen lamp in a plate for the whole night. This sort of appeasement for the procurement of child is known as 'Jagran' or 'Dardeo'. There is a popular belief among the Bhotias that a child born during the 'Amawasya' (Dark phase of the moon) causes hardships to himself or his parents.

They have discussed the obstetrical practice among the Bhotia tribals. The Bhotias use very simple and unhygienic method to expel the placenta, locally known as 'Phali', from the mother's womb after child-birth, if it is not expelled in natural course. The Bhotia women are also given a gentle abdominal massage and tea brewed from the 'Bodpa' leaves, found in Tibet, to effect easy delivery of the child.

AHI (2000) in its report on National profile on women, Health and Development highlights the profile of women, health and development with emphasis on the links missing between women, health and development. This needs to be addressed by the National Health Policy and a policy on women's health. All policies and programmes should be carefully designed and effectively implemented.

NAHI (2002) in its report on health and development challenges of Chhatisgarh, Jharkhand and Uttaranchal presented the analysis of health situation, RCH, health development and issues of NGO participation and development agenda. The analysis is based on statistics thrown out by National Family health Survey II, 1998-99, census, reports, RCH household survey II, 1999, etc.

Mishra *et.al.* (2003) in their India Health Report highlighted the issues of heath scenario, state role in health development, economic growth, poverty and equitable health, communicable diseases, maternal and child survival, HIV/ AIDS non-communicable diseases, private health care, public health care, health financier, health resent etc. They lamented upon the health deprivation of the poor and the burden of private sector in health services. They raised the issues of emerging challenges in health sector and demanded a clear-cut health policy.

Planning Commission in its report on health care for women and children for the Tenth Five Year Plan highlighted the burden of diseases, RCH services, family welfare infrastructure, involvement of NGO, and presented a package of policy recommendation for the Plan Period. The report concluded by stating that strategies and programmes followed till now have taken a rather narrow perspective on the health of women and children. Women's health programmes have been primarily designed to address issues related maternal health, child health interventions have focused on mortality prevention with insufficient emphasis on development issues. Hence the Tenth Plan would aim more holistic view of health of women and children to include intervention, other than those directly related to reproductive health of women.

Srinivasan (2004) has visualized the health care in India. He discussed the key achievements in health sector, major disease control efforts, health infrastructure in private sector, health financing issues etc. Similarly, Ramchandran visualizes health, nutrition and population scenario in 2020. He discussed health status, health care system, human resources development, preventive health system, financing health care, National Health Policy, 2002, family welfare etc.

Saroj Pachauri (2002) in her edited volume on Implemented A Reproductive Health Agenda In India presented reproductive health profile of adolescent girls, maternal care practices, community based programmes for adolescent girls, women and role of NGO's in reproductive health. A number of programmes in the voluntary sector have attempted to address the issue of RTI's within their integrated approach to women's health. The approach has largely depended on the programmes philosophy, available resources and their priorities in the light of other equally pressing issues that may need to be addressed. Some are essentially clinic-based programmes, providing allopathic treatment. Others are exclusively community based awareness raising, holding sporadic gynecological camps, training their community-based health workers in the syndrome management of the common RTI's such as using herbal remedies.

Renu Khanna etal (2002) in her edited volume on Comprehensive Women's Health Programmes and Policy highlighted the issues of primary health care marks involvement in women's health, functioning of women's health programmes, women's health policies and programmes, decentralized planning and implemented of RCH services etc.

Agnihotri (2003) has presented in depth analysis of sex ratios from census reports. He has lamented upon the declining trend of sex ratio in the age group of 0 to 6 years.

Sudha and Rajan (2003) have examined the sex ratios at birth and child mortality in India. They have also examined determinants of persistent daughter disadvantages.

Santhya and Jejeebhoy (2003) have examined the issue of sexual and reproductive health status of married adolescent girls. They have advocated for better understanding of the needs of sexual and reproductive health of married adolescent girl for improving the health status of women and children.

The review of literature simply demonstrates that there is paucity of empirical data, literature and information on dynamics of health and care services in the state of Uttar Pradesh and Uttaranchal. Moreover, most of the studies are dealing with specific issues and concentrate in specific region. Thus, the present study is an attempt to fill this gap and analyse the dynamics of health and care of women and children in northern India, particularly in the states of Uttar Pradesh and Uttaranchal.

RELEVANCE OF THE STUDY

Though India has never had a clear cut policy for women and children health, a range of policy decisions has directly or indirectly influenced women and children health. The focus of health programmes and policy was on the family planning programmes but since this has now acquired a Reproductive and Child Health slant, women's reproductive health is now an official concern. However, women's health covers much more than their occupational and reproductive health. A comprehensive policy on women's health as a strong component of the overall National Health Policy is thus urgently needed. The review of policies and programmes delineates the main constraints of the planning process that more serious implications for women's health. Though the Indian family welfare programme had much strength, such as its size and the number of services provided, its main weakness is more inadequate population coverage and poor service quality. Contraceptive targets were particularly blamed for poor service quality because they diverted the attention of the health staff away from health services. While, under the RCH programme, the Indian government committed to providing a package of reproductive services such as safe delivery, pre and post- natal care, abortion, treatment of reproductive tract infections (RTI's) and sexually transmitted diseases (STD's), counseling on sexuality and responsible parenthood, and contraceptive services. Some of these services are currently available, some need strengthening, and some are to be newly introduced in the programme. It was envisaged that the service package would be delivered through local health planning, improving service quality and increasing client satisfaction. However, women in the northern states have relatively little autonomy in terms of freedom of movement, inheritance rights, control over economic resources, and support from their natal home after marriage. Women in these states are more vulnerable and powerless and therefore suffer more from higher fertility and mortality. In addition to lack of autonomy, their lack of knowledge and awareness about reproductive health are other factors that determine the quality of care they get and the preventive measures they can take. Again, administrative constraints and procedural bottlenecks, which hamper the smooth functioning of the programme, need to be tackled urgently. This will require system reforms. Thus, the present study is expected to provide the desired database and insights for formulating action plan and policy measures for enhancing the effective, efficiency and wider impact of the programme, ensuring community and private sector participation.

OBJECTIVES OF STUDY

The study has the following main objectives:

(i) to review plan, policies and programmes of women and children's health status and health care and also to highlight the nutritional status of women and girl children.

(ii) to assess the needs of sexual and reproductive health of married adolescent and also to assess the access and participation of women and children in RCH services.

(iii) to study the determinants of persistent daughter disadvantage and to examine sex ratio's patterns among the population.

(iv) to study the infant and child mortality rates and also to examine the problem of female infanticides.

(v) to examine the problems, constraints, and challenges in administering women and child health programme and health care for women and children;

(vi) to examine the role of ICDS in promoting the health care and improving health status of women and children;

(vii) to suggest policy measures for improving women and adolescent girls' health status, reducing mortality rates, enhancing effectiveness and efficiency of health care programmes for women and children and proper functioning of existing health programmes.

HYPOTHESIS TO BE TESTED

The following hypotheses have been empirically tested:

(i) The existing health staff, resources and outreach of the health infrastructure are insufficient to support even the current health programmes.

(ii) Community participation in health care programmes is low due to lack of efforts for community mobilization, gender sensitization and poor level of awareness regarding, existing health care programme.

(iii) Poor health status of pregnant and lactating mothers is affecting the health and nutrition of infant as well as low level of immunization and vaccination is causing high mortality rate among girl children.

(iv) The functioning of government run health programmes as well as health facilities is not satisfactory. Even persons from disadvantaged classes prefer to visit and receive treatment from private health practitioners and hospitals on heavy cost.

(v) Decentralization of health services and delegation of the latter to women's groups and organizations may be an effective way to reach health care to the poorest populations.

(vi) Combination of a strong grass-root base with policy action can help in the development of health policies and programmes that reflect the health priorities of poor women.

METHODOLOGY

The study is empirical in nature and based on mainly primary data collected from field survey. Field survey has been conducted in Uttar Pradesh and Uttaranchal. A sample of 3 districts in each state has been selected to cover 600 households. The selection of districts and areas is based on random procedure. The selection of households is also based on random procedure; however, levels of development have been the main criteria of selection of areas and households. Udham Singh Nagar, Pithoragarh, Dehradoon from Uttaranchal and Azamgarh, Jhansi and Sitapur from Uttar Pradesh have been selected for field survey.

The household survey has been conducted with the help of structured interview schedules for households and health functionaries. The health functionaries, representatives of local NGOs, community based organizations and para-medical staff, administrative staff of hospitals and dispensaries etc. have been interviewed. The schedule pertain the research questions, points and scales of view perceptions related to socio-economic and cultural setting, belief and value system, status of health diseases, nutrition, health behaviour, health practices, demographic transition etc. Major research and academic institutes, medical colleges and health and medical departments have been visited frequently for gathering of data and interaction with functionaries' experts, officials and development activists for insight stimulation on the topic of investigation. Moreover, websites of different organizations, departments and agencies will be searched for collection of data and statistics pertaining to health, medical disease, eco-system, cultural settings, value system, tribal development programmes, magico-religious belief system and other related issues.

Besides, secondary data and pertinent literature has been surveyed from published and documented sources. Previous studies, surveys, reports and documents have been consulted and reviewed accordingly for insight stimulation on the topic of investigation. The filled in schedules have been processed in computer through the use of statistical tool and techniques for drawing out inferences, results and conclusions. The data in tabulated form has been analyzed and interpreted. The policy measures are based on the critical appreciation of pertinent literature and analysis of research findings.

SCOPE OF THE STUDY

The Study is confined to Uttar Pradesh and Uttaranchal, however, analysis of secondary data and pertinent literature has been ensured in the national perspective. Interstate analysis of data and research findings analysis of data and research findings has enhanced the scope of the present study. Moreover, study is useful for formulation of micro-plans for improving health status of women and their children.

2

HEALTH CARE SERVICES FOR WOMEN AND CHILDREN

Countries like China and Sri lanka have demonstrated that maternal and child health status can be improved tremulously though community initiatives, with existing economic growth of the country. Better governance, improvement in female education, proper facility for safe drinking water and sanitation, containing both indoor and out door pollution, gender equity, and access to affordable health care facilities has considerable impact in improving the health and nutritional status of women and children. It is utmost of importance, other wise; country will trap into the of vicious cycle of low productivity and poverty. India's more than 60% of the total population is represented by women in the reproductive age group (15-45 yrs) and children (<15 yrs). Additionally, one fifth of the population is of adolescent age group and their reproductive span will continue to grow. Thus populations in the reproductive age as well as the need for more funds is bound to rise in the coming years. Hence prioritizing maternal and child health care interventions becomes challenging. To reach out to the bottom 300-400 million people who perceive health services unavailable and inaccessible is a tough task to tackle as well.

TYPES OF HEALTH CARE

Broadly health care may be divided into three categories i.e. (a) Informal Health Care; (b) Interface Health Care; and (c) Formal Health Care (Mishra, 2004).

(a) **Informal Health Care:** It is provided by non-professionals such as family members for whom these activities do not constitute an occupation, at least not a paid one. At the functional level, illness provides an occasion for reinforcing solidarity amongst relatives, friends and all others concerned; treatment is medicated through cultural mechanisms which interact with biological factors. In this form of health care, the important elements are self-care, family, and the community.

(b) **Interface Health Care:** Some occupations are on the borderline. These are traditional healer is, pharmacists in drug stores etc. They work for pay, but are not scientifically trained, although they may have a wealth of experience and shrewd perceptions of what treatment will work in a particular case.

(c) **Formal Health Care:** It can be provided by a variety of professionals (from various systems of medicine)-nurses, physical therapists and physicians etc.

Some of the components of health are shown in Table 1. There are several factors, which influence the health status. These factors are shown in Table 2.

Table 1
Components of Health

	Absence of Disease	*Absence of Ill Health*	*Presence of Positive Health (well-being)*
Physical Health	Long life No Physical disease Low-risk of disease Low-risk lifestyle	No physical symptoms No physical disability	Fitness Health-promoting lifestyle
Mental Health	No psychiatric disease	No mental distress No mental disability	Self-esteem Mental ability Resilience
Social Health	No social/family breakdown	No social/family frictions	Role in society Social support Sense of belonging

Table 2
Major Influences on Health

Genetic makeup	*Influence*
Basic needs	Warmth and Shelter, Food and Water, Freedom from Physical Violence
Physical environment	Housing, Drinking Water/Sewerage Air Quality, Food Quality and Safety, Roads, Transport, Noise Workplace
Lifestyle	Smoking, Eating, Drinking, Exercise, Illicit Drug Use, Safe Sex Practices, Use of Medical Services
Environmental constraints on lifestyle	Available Facilities (exercise, food choice in shops), Peer Pressure, Advertising, Cultural Pressures, Education

Improvement in the health status of the population has been one of the major thrust areas for the social development programmes of the country. This was to be achieved through improving the access to and utilization of health services with special focus on under-served and underprivileged segments of the population. Over the last five decades, India has built up a vast health infrastructure and manpower at primary, secondary and tertiary care in Government, voluntary and private sectors. Professionals and paraprofessionals trained in the medical colleges in modern medicine and ISM & H and paraprofessional training institution man these institutions. The population has become aware of the benefits of health-related technologies for prevention, early diagnosis and effective treatment for a wide variety of illnesses and accessed available services. Technological advances and improvement in access to health care technologies, which were relatively inexpensive and easy to implement, had resulted in substantial improvement in health indices of the population and a steep decline in mortality (Table 3).

The extent of access to and utilization of health care varied substantially between states, districts and different segments of society; this to a large extent, is responsible for substantially differences between states in health indices of the population.

During the 1990s, the mortality rates reached a plateau and the country entered an era of dual disease burden.

Communicable diseases have become more difficult to combat because of development of insecticide resistant strains of vectors, antibiotics resistant strains of bacteria and emergence of HIV infection for which there is no therapy. Longevity and changing life style have resulted in the increasing prevalence of non-communicable diseases. Under nutrition, micro nutrient deficiencies and associated health problems coexist with obesity and non-communicable diseases. The existing health system suffers from inequitable distribution of institutions and manpower. Even though the country produces over 17,000 doctors in modern system of medicine and similar number of ISM&H practitioners and paraprofessionals, there are huge gaps in critical manpower in institutions providing primary healthcare, especially in the remote rural and tribal areas where health needs are the greatest (Ramchandran, 2004).

Table 3
Growth (1951-2000) in Health Care Services

	1951	*1981*	*2001*
SC/PHC/CHC	725	57,363	1,63,181 (99-RHS)
Dispensaries & Hospitals (all)	9209	23,555	43,322 (95-96-CBHI)
Beds (Pvt. & Public)	117,198	569495	8,70,161 (95-96-CBHI)
Doctors (Modern System)	18,054	1,43,887	7,37,000 (98-99-MCI)
Nursing Personnel	61,800	2,68,700	5,03,900 (99-INC)
Malaria (cases in million)	75	2.7	2.2
Leprosy (cases/10,000 population)	38.1	57.3	3.74
Small Pox (no. of cases)	>44,887	Eradicated	
Guinea worm (no. of cases)		>39,792	Eradicated
Polio (no. of cases)		29709	265
Life Expectancy (years)	36.7	54	64.6 (RGI)
Crude Birth Rate	40.8	33.9 (SRS)	26.1 (99 SRS)
Crude Death Rate	25	12.5 (SRS)	8.7 (99 SRS)
IMR	146	110	70 (99 SRS)

Source: National Health Policy-2002.

As the country undergoes demographic and epidemiological transition, it is likely that larger investments in health will be needed even to maintain the current health status because tackling resistant infections and non-communicable diseases will inevitably lead to escalating health care costs. Last two decades have witnessed explosive expansion in expensive health care related technologies and broadening of diagnostic and therapeutic avenues. Increasing awareness and rising expectations to access these have widened the gap between what is possible and what is affordable for the individual or the country. Policy makers and programme managers realise that in order to address the increasingly complex situation regarding access to good quality care at affordable costs, it is essential to build up an integrated health system with appropriate screening, regulating access at different levels and referral linkages. However, both health care providers and health care seekers still feel more comfortable with the one-to-one relationship than with the health system approach.

Another problem is the popular perception that curative and preventive care compete for available resources, with the former getting preference in funding. Efforts to convince the public that preventive and curative care are both part of the entire spectrum of health care ranging from health promotion, specific protection, early diagnosis and prompt treatment, disability limitation and rehabilitation and that to improve the health status of the population both are equally essential have not been very successful. Traditionally, health service (both government and private) was perceived as a social responsibility albeit a paid one. Growing commercialization of health care and medical education over the last two decades has eroded this commitment, adversely affecting the quality of care, trust and the rapport between health care seekers and providers.

Costs of treatment and affordability are crucial in determining women's access to health care especially in poorer groups. The availability of finances is linked not only to utilisation of private facilities but to levels of non-utilisation. Women, in particular, would use public facilities more if these were not so severely dysfunctional or if they were more patient-friendly. As it is, there would be expenditure even to access care in public hospitals. None of the health expenditure studies provides separate break ups of costs incurred in the public and private sector. Expenditure on medicines and doctors fees generally formed a sizeable chunk of total expenditure even in those States that show very high levels of public sector utilisation for patient care (Sundar, 1995). Some of the evidence available show:

- Women and men tended to depend on public hospitals where costs were significantly lower. In 1993, more than 60% of the men and women using hospital facilities went to public hospitals.
- Hundred per cent utilisation of public hospital facilities were found in rural West Bengal, rural Himachal Pradesh as well as rural and urban Assam and urban Rajasthan.
- There was less than 50% utilisation of public hospitals in States like Gujarat, Maharashtra, Andhra Pradesh and Tamil Nadu where there was a dominant presence of private hospitals.
- Significantly, fewer women went to hospital.
- Expenditure incurred on the treatment of women tended to be lower than that incurred on the males in the household despite greater morbidity amongst women. Except in the case of acute illnesse this difference was significant for all categories of illnesses treated in and outside a hospital environment in 1993.
- A study in rural Punjab showed significantly lower costs on the medical care of lower birth order girls (Das Gupta, 1987).

STATUS OF HEALTH

Health infrastructure is shown in Table 4. There are 18.5 beds per lakh of population in rural areas and 232.36 beds per lakh of population in urban areas. Thus, there are 73.71 beds per lakh of population. The health infrastructure is found to be in favour of urban areas.

As per 1998-99, NFHS-II survey, 20 per cent mothers receive antenatal care while only 33.6 per cent births are delivered in medical institution. Only 42.3 per cent deliveries are being assisted by health professional. The states like Bihar, Rajasthan,

Table 4
State-wise Health Infrastructure In India (As on Jan. 1996)

Sl. No.	States	Rural			Urban			Total		
		Hospitals	Beds	Beds per lakh of population	Hospitals	Beds	Beds per lakh of population	Hospitals	Beds	Beds per lakh of population
1.	Andhra Pradesh	883	10,117	20.81	2007	35,715	199.67	2890	45,832	68.91
2.	Assam	151	3949	19.82	117	8712	350.16	268	12,661	56.49
3.	Bihar	100	3018	4.02	228	26,072	229.65	328	29,090	33.68
4.	Gujarat	179	5798	21.42	2349	57,619	404.46	2528	63,417	153.51
5.	Haryana	8	543	4.38	71	6637	163.67	79	7180	43.61
6.	Himachal P.	19	549	11.63	38	4519	1005.46	57	5068	98.01
7.	Karnataka	25	3015	9.7	268	35,434	251.77	293	38,449	85.49
8.	Kerala	1443	44,103	205.92	597	33,096	430.94	2040	77,199	265.3
9.	M.P.	245	6128	12.05	118	11,959	77.96	363	18,087	27.41
10.	Maharashtra	469	10,209	21.1	2646	68,711	224.97	3115	78,920	99.98
11.	Orissa	287	5115	18.65	143	9769	230.67	430	14,884	47.01
12.	Punjab	75	2330	16.31	145	12,491	208.43	220	14,821	73.07
13.	Rajasthan	14	1150	3.39	204	20,037	199.04	218	21,187	48.15
14.	Tamil Nadu	89	4235	11.51	319	44,545	233.49	408	48,780	87.33
15.	Uttar Pradesh	83	2585	2.32	652	44,693	161.9	735	47,278	33.99
16.	West Bengal	112	6352	12.37	287	48,878	261.27	399	55,230	81.13
17.	India	4621	122,453	18.5	10,416	501,366	232.36	15,037	623,819	73.71

Source: Health Information of India, 1995 and 1996 CBHI, MHFW; Census of India, 1991.

Uttar Pradesh and Madhya Pradesh have shown poor health status as per health indicators (Table 5).

Table 5
State-wise Maternal Care Indicators In India (1998-99)

India/State	*Percentage who received all recommended types of antenatal care (1)*	*Percentage of births delivered in a medical institution*	*Percentage of deliveries assisted by a health professional (2)*	*Percentage of non-institutional deliveries with a post-partum check-up within two months of birth (3)*	*Percentage of non-institutional deliveries with a post-partum check-up within two days of birth (3)*
India	20.0	33.6	42.3	16.5	2.3
Andhra Pradesh	35.6	49.8	65.2	44.9	1.6
Bihar	6.4	14.6	23.4	10.0	1.4
Gujarat	25.0	46.3	53.5	10.4	1.6
Haryana	20.8	22.4	42.0	15.7	2.5
Jammu & Kashmir	30.7	35.6	42.4	27.6	1.1
Karnataka	41.5	51.1	59.1	35.3	3.6
Kerala	64.9	93.0	94.0	27.4	7.5
Madhya Pradesh	10.9	20.1	29.7	10.0	0.5
Maharashtra	31.0	52.6	59.4	29.8	6.9
Orissa	21.4	22.6	33.4	19.2	2.2
Punjab	31.7	37.5	62.6	20.3	5.7
Rajasthan	8.3	21.5	35.8	6.4	0.5
Tamil Nadu	50.8	79.3	83.8	53.0	10.1
Uttar Pradesh	4.4	15.5	22.4	7.2	1.5
West Bengal	19.7	40.1	44.2	31.6	7.1

Note: Table includes only the two most recent births during the three years preceding the survey.

1. Three or more antenatal check-ups (with the first check-up within the first trimester of pregnancy), two or more tetanus toxoid injections, and iron and folic acid tablets or syrup for three or more months.
2. Doctor, auxiliary nurse midwife, nurse, midwife, lady health visitor, or other health professional.
3. Based on births in the 2-35 months preceding the survey.

Source: IIPS and ORC Macro (2000). National Family Health Survey (NFHS-2), 1998-99, India. Mumbai: IIPS.

The percentage of pregnant women receiving two doses of tetanus toxoid vaccine is shown in Table 6. Only 53.8 per cent women receive these doses of tetanus toxoid vaccine, while it is reported as low as 28.3 per cent in Rajasthan followed by Bihar (30.7 per cent) and Uttar Pradesh (37.4 per cent). The percentage of women receiving antenatal checkup by health professional is shown in Table 7.

Table 6
Variation Across States on Essential Maternal Health

States	*Institutional delivery*	*There ore more ANC Check-up*
Andhra Pradesh	59.1	88.0
Assam	26.4	44.9
Bihar	20.2	18.2
Jharkhand	21.6	33.5
Gujarat	52.3	58.0
Haryana	32.4	44.4
Karnataka	58.2	81.9
Kerala	95.7	96.3
Madhya Pradesh	29.1	35.0
Chattisgarh	18.6	43.6
Maharashtra	57.6	71.0
Orissa	30.5	46.2
Punjab	43.1	62.7
Rajasthan	27.9	33.3
Tamil Nadu	87.4	96.8
Uttar Pradesh	22.2	27.3
West Bengal	51.8	64.9
All India	46.9	56.1

Source: DLHS 2002-03 MoHFW.

STATUS OF CHILD HEALTH

There exists a very strong positive correlation between maternal health care received and maternal mortality. Across, plan periods and various national and state level Programs implemented for maternal health care, stressed the need for screening of pregnant women for identifying the high risk cases and operationalizing a functional essential and emergency obstetric care ensuring better antenatal care for women.

However, even now there has been only a marginal percentage increase in number of women who are able to utilize the institutional delivery services and ante-natal care facilities. The table 6 demonstrates the regional variations across the states that call for state/region specific interventions for a favorable pregnancy outcome.

Over the decades, the trends in infant mortality rate (IMR) show a slow, but steady decline from 134 in 1951 to 60 per live births in 2003. It is estimated that around 30% of babies born are underweight (<2500gm) and this trend has not changed for the last few decades. Malnourished children are more prone to deaths. Research studies carried out within the country as well as abroad demonstrate, important and effective interventions, that play a major role in reduction of IMR these are: (i) Home based new born care (Gadchiroli model, Dr. Antia model etc., (ii) exclusive breastfeeding upto 6 months (iii) pneumonia and diarrhoea management (iv) strengthening of the immunization Program focusing on six vaccine preventable diseases, along with pulse polio Program and (v) increased dissemination of Oral Rehydration Salt (ORS). As these interventions would get significance while examining the information pertaining to various causes of child mortality.(i.e. Neo-natal causes forms 37%, Diarrhoea(17%), pneumonia(19%), malaria(8%), measles (4%), injuries(3%), HIV/AIDS(3%) and others (10%)).

Table 7 displays, how the coverage of childcare strategies varies across the states. The simplest intervention for breast feeding to the baby varies from 9.2% in Bihar to 84% in Chattisgarh. In states like Bihar, Jharkhand and Orissa, which are economically weak and with poor healthcare infrastructure facilities, can take, appropriate steps to enhance this tried and tested low cost intervention in a larger way through proper IEC activities to improve the health and nutritional status of children. States like Maharashtra and Tamil Nadu can also appropriately utilize this strategy by imparting education to mothers.

Even though India is spending huge amount of funds on routine immunization in general and pulse polio in particular full immunization coverage has not gone beyond 90% except in Tamil Nadu. In five states (Assam, Bihar, Jharkhand, Rajasthan and Uttar Pradesh), the immunization coverage is as low as i.e. less than 30%. It is also noteworthy to see that these are the states where infant deaths also happen in huge numbers. Another reason that can be attributed to low coverage may be high drop out for measles vaccination.

Table 7
Variation Across States on Essential Child Care Health

States	*Women who gave exclusive breast milk for at least 4 months to their child (%)*	*% of Children who received*		*Given ORS to children with diarrhoea (%)*
		Measles	*Full Immunization*	
Andhra Pradesh	75.0	74.8	61.9	81.4
Assam	53.1	47.3	21.5	33.4
Bihar	9.2	26.1	23.1	31.9
Jharkhand	10.4	32.2	26.0	36.5
Gujarat	27.4	72.3	58.0	72.9
Haryana	72.4	68.5	60.4	72.3
Karnataka	68.0	81.9	76.2	84.7
Kerala	51.8	89 0	82.5	92.0
Madhya Pradesh	49.7	52.6	33.6	51.4
Chattisgarh	84.3	65.6	57.5	67.7
Maharashtra	30.7	89.6	70.9	78.7
Orissa	45.4	70.5	55.3	70.8
Punjab	74.1	83.2	78.5	85.0
Rajasthan	24.1	35.9	24.6	38.6
Tamil Nadu	48.6	96.2	94.0	97.2
Uttar Pradesh	52.0	38.8	29.4	38.5
West Bengal	41.4	69.6	54.0	81.4
All India	56.1	64.5	49.5	60.8

Source: DLHS 2002-03 MoHFW.

Pneumonia and Measles along with Diarrhoea together form major causes of deaths among children in India. Pneumonia is an infection of the lungs, and can be caused by bacteria, viruses and fungi. Pneumonia can be effectively managed through antibiotics and proper medical interventions such as hospitalization and oxygen support.

Diarrhoea, second leading fatal disease is common among children, especially those between 6 months and two years of age. It is also common in babies under the age of six months who are fed with breast milk substitutes. With more than 50% of children below 5 years are moderately & severely undernourished and these already malnourished children are doubly cursed when they have to face diarrhoea. Though, Diarrhoea is a killer disease, it can be completely brought under control through appropriate interventions and maintenance of certain preventive practices which include breast feeding, improved weaning, personal hygiene, safe sanitation, potable drinking water and immunization against measles.

Diarrhoea management (giving ORS to children with diarrhoea), in earlier indicated five states, is also very poor i.e. less than 40% coverage. These data point out the non-effectiveness of various child health care strategies in these states calling for modification and reorientation of the strategies especially in these states.

Poor nutritional status is also a potent risk factor for neonatal, infant and child mortality. National Family Health Survey (1998-1999) categorised 47 per cent children below three years of age as under-nourished and 45 per cent as stunted. Also, it is estimated that one-third of all infants are born with low birth weight (<2.5 kg). Over the past five decades, India has achieved 50 per cent *decline in mortality* but has been unable to bring about reductions in *under-nutrition* beyond 20 per cent. Thus improving nutritional status of children is also an important agenda, which calls for urgent attention.

There are wide gaps in antenatal care in rural and urban areas. Urban women receive more antenatal care services as compared to rural women. The home visit by health worker during pregnancy is found to be very low. Only 21 per cent women reported that health workers visited them. However, 24.3 per cent rural women reported health workers visited them during their pregnancy. The low response was reported in Punjab, Haryana, Bihar and Rajasthan.

It is to be noted that majority of the people prefer private health services rather than utilizing government services. It is because of the fact that government health services entail high costs, and lack timely supply of drugs, facilities and care (Table 8 and 9). Only half of the pregnant women received iron and folic acid tablets during their pregnancy. Even this was found as low as 21.4 per cent in Bihar and 29.2 per cent in Rajasthan.

Table 8
Utilisation of Health Services for Illness within the Preceding Three Months in India (Per cent)

Service	*Andhra Pradesh*	*Bihar*	*Gujarat*	*Uttar Pradesh*
Government	20.2	24.4	53.8	6.2
Private	69.5	62.9	27.0	80.8
No treatment or home treatment	10.3	12.7	19.2	13.0

Source: For Bihar and Gujarat, ICMR (1988a); for Andhra Pradesh and Uttar Pradesh, ORG (1990).

Table 9
Reasons for Dissatisfaction with Government Health Services

Reason	*Andhra Pradesh*	*Bihar*	*Gujarat*	*Uttar Pradesh*
High Costs of staff or drugs	23	63	4	62
Travel Costs: Distances	5	50	91	28
Lack of supplies, drugs, facilities	23	35	60	62
Long Waits	11	7	11	8
Absence of Staff	–	13	5	–

Note: Percentage may exceed 100 because of answers N.L -: Not available.
Source: For Bihar and Gujarat, ICMR (1998a); for Uttar Pradesh, ORG (1988c)

In Uttar Pradesh, only 29.5 per cent pregnant women received iron and folic acid tablets during their pregnancy (Table 10).

The women were asked regarding their delivery of pregnancy. Institutional delivery of pregnancies is still very low. Rajasthan, Orissa, Uttar Pradesh, Bihar and Madhya Pradesh reported very low response in institutional delivery of pregnancies. The coverage of antenatal check up has been found to be low in most of the states (Table 11).

Table 10
Coverage of Antenatal Check up among Pregnant Women in India

State	*Percentage receiving iron and folic acid tablets*	*1998–99*				
		Weight Taken	*BP Taken*	*Abor–tion*	*IFA Given*	*At Least one TT*
India	50.5	34.5	38.2	49.4	48.7	74.7
Kerala	91.2	83.0	96.0	87.8	90.0	95.7
Tamil Nadu	84.1	89.2	87.5	89.3	79.1	98.3
Andhra Pradesh	76.4	54.3	67.1	82.4	72.6	83.0
Karnataka	74.9	33.9	47.4	64.9	42.7	88.5
Punjab	73.6	66.0	65.5	79.7	76.8	89.5
Maharashtra	70.6	66.0	65.6	79.7	76.8	89.5
Gujarat	69.3	40.7	43.7	53.0	68.1	77.0
Haryana	59.9	27.5	30.6	50.1	48.1	81.0
West Bengal	56.3	46.8	47.9	48.9	54.7	86.4
Orissa	49.9	27.3	28.6	43.8	60.8	79.7
Madhya Pradesh	44.3	17.8	19.9	40.1	45.3	69.8
Uttar Pradesh	29.5	8.0	10.0	25.7	27.7	60.5
Rajasthan	29.2	13.2	19.9	33.5	34.5	62.0
Bihar	21.4	11.8	16.2	25.4	16.9	64.6

Note: States are listed in descending order of coverage.
Source: NFHS–I and II, IIPS, Bombay

The CPR is also found to be very low in the states of Bihar, Rajasthan, UP and Madhya Pradesh. The unmet need of family planning is about 19.5 per cent but it is highly reported in UP, Bihar, Orissa, MP and Rajasthan (Table 12).

Due to poor access to health services, pregnant women suffer problems of anemia and high mortality rate. The proportion of anemia is found high in the age group of 15-19 years (56 per cent) followed by 20-24 years (53.8 per cent) while severe anemia was reported high in the age group of 15-45 years (Table 13).

Table 11
Place of Delivery and Delivery Attendance in India

State	*Institution*						*Not in Institution*		
	Public		*Private*		*Total*		*Other health profe-ssional*	*TBA*	*Other*
	Doctor	*Other*	*Doctor*	*Other*	*Doctor*	*Other*			
India	9.8	4.9	9.4	1.5	25.6	2.4	6.7	35.1	30.2
Tamil Nadu	17.8	15.9	24.3	5.6	63.6	0.5	7.9	21.2	6.8
Gujarat	9.5	5.7	16.3	4.1	35.7	2.8	4.7	44.9	11.9
Maharashtra	13.4	9.4	18.0	3.4	44.1	2.4	7.4	19.9	26.1
Kerala	33.8	5.2	46.4	3.1	88.4	0.2	1.6	8.3	1.4
Punjab	7.1	2.7	11.9	3.1	24.8	4.1	19.5	49.6	2.1
Karnataka	13.9	7.8	13.6	2.3	37.6	3.0	10.8	21.8	26.8
Andhra Pradesh	11.4	2.3	17.9	1.3	33.0	7.1	10.1	33.8	16.1
Haryana	6.4	2.8	6.3	1.2	16.7	4.7	9.2	66.2	3.1
Bihar	4.4	1.4	5.5	0.8	12.1	2.8	4.3	58.2	22.6
Madhya Pradesh	8.6	3.4	3.2	0.8	16.0	2.2	12.3	29.8	39.7
West Bengal	13.7	12.6	4.6	0.7	31.5	1.8	0.5	36.2	30.0
Uttar Pradesh	5.3	1.7	3.7	0.6	11.3	0.9	5.3	33.3	49.1
Orissa	9.2	2.9	1.8	0.3	14.2	2.0	4.9	37.3	41.7
Rajasthan	6.9	2.6	1.7	0.3	11.6	2.6	8.1	40.5	37.2

Note: TBA, traditional birth attendants. States are listed in descending order of institutional delivery.
Source: NFHS–I and II, IIPS, Bombay.

Table 12
Unmet Need for Family Planning in India

State	*Unmet Need (%)*	*State*	*Unmet Need (%)*
India	19.5	Karnataka	18.2
Uttar Pradesh	30.1	West Bengal	17.4
Bihar	25.1	Haryana	16.4
Orissa	22.4	Tamil Nadu	14.6
Madhya Pradesh	20.5	Maharashtra	14.1
Rajasthan	19.8	Gujarat	13.1
Andhra Pradesh	10.4	Punjab	13.0

Note: The unmet need for family planning service is defined at the percentage of couples not desiring additional children and not practicing family planning. States are listed in descending order of unmet need.
Source: IIPS (1995).

Table 13
Per cent of Women Suffering from Anemia

Age	*Total*	*Mild*	*Moderate*	*Severe*
Pregnant Women 15-45	49.7	21.8	25.4	2.5
Women 15-45	51.8	35.0	14.8	1.9
Women 15-19	56.0	36.2	17.9	1.9
Women 20-24	53.8	34.8	17.0	2.0
Women 25-29	51.4	34.8	14.7	1.9
Women 30-34	50.5	34.8	13.7	1.9
Women 35-49	50.5	35.1	13.6	1.9

Source: NFHS-II, 1998-99, IIPS, Mumbai.

Table 14
Early Neonatal Morality Rates and Percentage Share of Early Neonatal Deaths to Infant Deaths by Residence, in India

	Early neo-natal mortality			*Early neo-natal deaths as Percentage of infant deaths*		
	Total	*Rural*	*Urban*	*Total*	*Rural*	*Urban*
India*	35	37	23	48.6	48.3	50.5
Andhra Pradesh	38	41	29	58.4	56.0	74.9
Assam	36	37	20	47.5	47.2	54.1
Bihar	33	34	24	46.8	46.9	44.1
Gujarat	30	30	28	48.2	44.8	60.3
Haryana	31	31	29	45.5	44.8	49.0
Himachal Pradesh	32	33	19	50.5	50.4	51.4
Karnataka	33	41	13	62.4	63.9	52.3
Kerala	8	8	8	55.9	58.5	49.8
Madhya Pradesh	47	48	36	48.4	47.5	59.4
Maharashtra	25	30	16	52.0	52.4	50.6
Orissa	44	45	31	46.0	45.9	48.0
Punjab	26	28	18	50.2	51.1	45.9
Rajasthan	44	46	30	51.0	51.2	49.3
Tamil Nadu	32	35	24	59.5	58.4	63.3
Uttar Pradesh	37	39	27	44.1	44.5	41.0
West Bengal	27	29	18	48.4	49.6	41.4

Source: NFHS-II, 1998-99, IIPS, Mumbai.

The neonatal mortality rates are shown in Table 14. The neonatal mortality rates are higher in rural areas as compared to urban areas. Again, they are higher in MP, Orissa, Rajasthan, UP and Andhra Pradesh. About half of the neonatal death occurs during early stage due to poor anemia, nutrition in take and lack of proper care. The child mortality rates are also higher in MP, UP, Rajasthan, and Bihar (Table 15).

Table 15
Child Mortality Rate

State	*Under-5 Mortality Rate*	*State*	*Under-5 Mortality Rate*
Kerala	19	Andhra Pradesh	86
Maharashtra	58	Assam	90
Tamil Nadu	63	India	95
West Bengal	68	Orissa	104
Karnataka	70	Bihar	105
Punjab	72	Rajasthan	115
Haryana	77	Uttar Pradesh	123
Himachal Pradesh	80	Madhya Pradesh	133
Gujarat	85		

Source: NFHS-II, 1998-99, IIPS, Mumbai.

Though there has been sharp decline in infant mortality rates during 1971 to 1998, however, it is still 72 per thousand live births. Neonatal mortality rates are higher than post-neonatal and prenatal mortality rates (Table 16).

Importantly, infant and child mortality rates are higher among SC's, ST's and low income groups (Table 17).

SRS estimates for 1997 also show high mortality rates for MP, Rajasthan, UP and Bihar (Table 18).

CAUSES OF MATERNAL MORTALITY

Data on major causes of maternal mortality is available from the SRS of the Registrar General of India. The major causes are ante and post-partum hemorrhage, anemia, obstructed labour, hypertensive disorders, post partum sepsis and unsafe abortions. SRS data reveals a reduction in deaths due to abortion from about 12 per cent in 1990 to 8.9 per cent in 1998, however, the trend with regard to other causes has by and large not changed significantly.

While deaths due to anemia, obstructed labour, hypertensive disorders and sepsis are preventable with

Table 16
Infant Mortality Indicators by Residence in India (1971-98)

Year	*Infant mortality rate*			*Neonatal mortality rate*			*Post-neonatal mortality rate*			*Perinatal mortality rate*		
	Total	*Rural*	*Urban*	*Total*	*Rural*	*Urban*	*Total*	*Rural*	*Urban*	*Total*	*Rural*	*Urban*
1971	129	138	82	75.2	80.6	45.4	54.2	57.4	36.6	53.4	56.7	35.6
1976	129	139	80	77.0	83.0	49.0	52.0	56.0	31.0	66.8	76.6	43.7
1981	110	119	63	69.9	75.6	38.5	40.5	43.5	24.0	54.6	58.8	31.5
1986	96	105	62	59.8	65.5	36.2	36.6	39.1	25.8	48.1	51.8	32.7
1990	80	86	50	52.5	57.4	30.9	27.2	28.9	19.5	48.4	51.7	34.0
1991	80	87	53	51.1	55.4	32.2	29.3	31.3	20.6	46.0	49.1	32.7
1992	79	85	53	50.0	53.6	33.0	29.4	31.4	20.0	47.5	50.3	34.0
1993	74	82	45	47.1	52.3	28.4	25.5	28.2	15.8	44.2	47.9	31.0
1994	74	80	52	47.7	52.0	32.6	26.0	27.5	19.6	42.5	43.4	38.7
1995	74	80	48	48.1	52.3	29.2	25.9	27.5	19.0	44.6	47.6	31.2
1996	72	77	46	47.0	50.0	28.0	25.0	27.0	17.0	44.0	46.0	32.0
1997	71	77	45	46.1	50.5	26.2	25.1	26.5	19.0	43.2	46.3	29.1
1998	72	77	45	45.0	49.0	27.0	27.0	28.0	18.0	42.0	45.0	29.0

$$\text{Perinatal rate} = \frac{\text{Number of still births and infant deaths of less 7 days during the year}}{\text{Number of live births and still births during the year}} \times 1000$$

Source: Registrar General (1999). Compendium of India's Fertility and Mortality Indicators 1971-97 (Based on the Sample Registration System), Office of the Registrar General, New Delhi.

Table 17
Infant and Child Mortality by Background Characteristics in India

Sl. No.	Background characteristics	NFHS-1 (1992-93)				NFHS-2 (1998-99)			
		Neo-natal mort.	Post-neonatal mort.	Infant mort.	Under-5 mort.	Neonatal mort.	Post-neonatal mort.	Infant mort.	Under-5 mort.
1.	Mother's Education								
	Illiterate	60.6	40.0	100.6	140.5	55.3	31.2	86.5	122.8
	Literate, <middle complete	38.8	23.7	62.5	83.9	40.5	18.0	58.5	75.8
	Middle school complete	37.6	18.5	56.1	64.8	33.7	14.4	48.1	58.1
	High School and above	25.3	11.9	37.2	43.2	24.3	8.5	32.8	37.1
2.	Caste/Tribe								
	Scheduled Caste	63.1	44.2	107.3	149.1	53.2	29.8	83.0	119.3
	Scheduled Tribe	54.6	35.9	90.5	135.2	53.3	30.9	84.2	126.6
	Other Backward Class	NA				50.8	25.2	76.0	103.1
	Others	50.6	31.6	82.2	111.5	40.7	21.2	61.8	82.6
3.	Medical Maternity Care								
	No antenatal or delivery care	57.5	39.3	96.8	145.8	53.6	35.5	89.1	Na
	Either antenatal or delivery care	41.2	22.5	63.7	85.1	35.8	19.0	54.8	NA
	Both antenatal and delivery care	29.8	14.5	44.2	56.8	22.2	11.8	34.0	NA
4.	Place of Delivery								
	Public health Facility	40.3	18.7	59.1	77.2	NA	NA	NA	NA
	Private Health Facility	27.5	11.0	38.5	42.3	NA	NA	NA	NA
	Home	46.5	30.9	77.5	114.3	NA	NA	NA	NA

Contd...

Sl. No.	Background characteristics	NFHS-1 (1992-93)				NFHS-2 (1998-99)			
		Neo-natal mort.	Post-neonatal mort.	Infant mort.	Under-5 mort.	Neonatal mort.	Post-neonatal mort.	Infant mort.	Under-5 mort.
5.	Religion								
	Hindu	55.0	35.4	90.4	124.0	50.4	26.7	77.1	107.0
	Muslim	47.1	29.6	76.6	106.3	38.0	20.8	58.8	82.7
	Christian	32.6	17.3	49.9	68.4	29.8	19.4	49.2	68.0
	Sikh	27.7	19.5	47.2	64.8	38.0	15.3	53.3	64.9
	Buddhist	36.6	19.8	56.4	99.3	39.5	14.0	53.6	66.9
6.	Standard of Living Index								
	Low	NA	NA	NA	NA	55.8	33.1	88.8	130.0
	Medium	NA	NA	NA	NA	47.0	23.4	70.3	94.6
	High	NA	NA	NA	NA	30.9	11.8	42.7	51.5
7.	Total	52.7	33.7	86.3	118.8	47.7	25.3	73.0	101.4

Note: In NFHS-2, medical are includes antenatal care received from a health worker, delivery assistance given by a doctor, nurse, trained midwife, or other health professional, and post-natal care received in a health facility or at home within two months of delivery. The three categories under medical maternity care in NFHS-2 are no care, one or two types of care, and all three types of care.

Source: 1. International Institute for Population Sciences (IIPS) (1995). National Family Health Survey, India, NFHS-1, 1992-93, Mumbai; IIPS. 2. International Institute for Population Sciences (IIPS) and ORC Macro (2000). National Family Health Survey (NFHS-2), 1998-99, India, Mumbai; IIPS.

Table 18
State-wise Maternal Mortality Rate in India

State/Area	*Indirect estimates 1982-86*			*SRS 1997*
	Maternal mortality ratio	*Maternal death rate**	*Percentage maternal deaths***	*of Maternal mortality rate*
India total	580	82	21	407***
India rural	638	96	22	NA
India urban	389	44	17	NA
Andhra Pradesh	394	50	13	159
Assam	1068	145	27	409
Bihar	813	139	27	452
Gujarat	373	51	15	28
Haryana	494	79	25	103
Karnataka	439	54	19	195
Kerala	247	21	15	198
Madhya Pradesh	507	84	21	498
Maharashtra	439	54	19	135
Orissa	844	113	24	367
Punjab	207	25	11	199
Rajasthan	627	110	29	670
Tamil Nadu	372	38	10	79
Uttar Pradesh	920	160	32	707
West Bengal	561	73	20	266

*Number of deaths per 100000 women in 15-49 age interval.
**Maternal deaths as percentage of all female deaths in 15-49 interval.
*** 95% CI for MMR estimate for India = 351 - 463.
*Sources:*SRS, 1997.

provision of adequate antenatal care, referral and timely treatment of complications of pregnancy, promoting institutional and safe delivery practices and postnatal care, hemorrhage during pregnancy is generally not predictable. These cases along with cases developing complications during deliveries conducted at homes and in PHCs require provision of adequate emergency obstetric care services and timely referrals to facilities equipped for handling such cases.

Maternal mortality is also affected by a wide range of socio-economic determinates, such as the status of women, low level of female education, economic dependency, lack of access to services and gender bias. Therefore, to reduce the current level of maternal mortality, besides providing for maternal health care services, it is necessary to improve the standard of education and social status of women (Planning Commission, 2001).

There are many shortcomings in the quality of mortality data available, and there is an immediate requirement to improve the quality of data inputs that are used for estimating disease burden.

From the data that has been presented, it can be concluded that for women, the major causes of burden are those related to their socio-economic vulnerability, specially in the age group 15-44 years. Neuro psychiatric morbidity and infectious diseases are also important causes of burden. Neoplasm's and ischemic heart disease form a significant component of burden in the elderly age group. Maternal *under-nutrition* contributes towards disease burden both in women and in children, as is shown in the high proportion of burden in infancy due to pre-natal mortality. The burden due to injuries in children is also high, as is the burden due to nutritional disorders and infectious diseases.

The Indian health scenario, admittedly presents daunting challenges. But, at the same time, it also presents great opportunities. The low base of health indicators combined with an overwhelming burden of avoidable morbidity and mortality accounted for by pre-transition diseases makes possible dramatic improvements in health status in a relatively short time-span. This presents a rare opportunity to the policy makers to rescue millions from the vicious cycle of sickness, high fertility, high mortality, and poverty. Of course, this would demand significantly enhanced public investment in health, at least to the modest level of 2.2 per cent of GDP- the average of lower-middle-income countries. This by itself requires more than doubling of the current level of public expenditure at around 1 per cent of GDP. Equally, it requires wide-ranging systemic reforms to ensure the efficient utilization of public resources to benefit the really needy and the poor (Planning Commission, 2001).

SCHEMES IN PLACE FOR MATERNAL AND CHILD HEALTH CARE

Maternal and Child Health (MCH) care services in India, are offered through a mix of public, private and volunteer health care delivery system. From the first plan period itself our Planners and implementers recognized the need for providing accessible, affordable, accountable and adequate health care facilities to the people. Maternal and child health programs have also undergone tremendous changes over past decades. Evolution of MCH programs dates back in 1952 the year on which Government of India adopted Family Planning Program. It took more than 40 years to have exclusive scheme/program for MCH related activities. In 1992, program named child survival and safe motherhood program (CSSM) introduced, to have focused agenda in addressing these issues. Cairo summit in 1994 reiterated the futility of addressing the health care needs of women and children in an isolated manner. In response to this, India initiated Reproductive and Child Health (RCH) program during ninth plan (1997-2001) period by revitalizing and strengthening the erstwhile CSSM Program.

However, some of the critical bottlenecks identified while implementing RCH-1 (1997-2005) are as follows:

- The move from centrally driven target-based planning to decentralized, community based planning needed the support of a strong decentralized planning process.
- Poor capacity to tailor the Program according to their requirement, by states.
- Range of multiple partners including donor agencies like USAID, UNICEF, WHO etc supporting stand alone project rather than taking an integrated approach.
- Poor monitoring and non- incentives for better performance.

All these components have a confounding effect on slow progress than expected. The ongoing RCH-II is expected to address theses issues while implementing the second phase of

RCH-II (2005-2010). In order to give a mission mode approach to encourage and enhance overall healthcare delivery system in the country, with a pro-poor approach Government of India launched National Rural Health Mission (NRHM) in April 2005. NRHM is envisaged for 7 years with a special focus on 18 states, (Arunachal Pradesh, Assam, Bihar, Chattisgarh, Himachal Pradesh, Jharkhand, Jammu and Kashmir, Manipur, Mizoram, Meghalaya, Madhya Pradesh, Nagaland, Orissa, Rajasthan, Sikkim, Tripura, Uttaranchal and Uttar Pradesh) which have weak public health indicators and/or weak infrastructure. The Mission aims to bridge the infirmities in rural healthcare through increased community ownership, decentralization of the programs to the district level, inter-sectoral convergence and improved primary health care. The Mission also aims to achieve the goals of the National Population Policy and the National Health Policy through improved access to affordable, accountable and reliable Primary Health Care.

NRHM envisages reduced IMR&MMR, universal access to public health services such as women's health, child health, water, sanitation & hygiene, immunization and nutrition, addressing both communicable and non-communicable diseases, including locally endemic diseases, population stabilization, gender and demographic balance, mainstreaming of AYUSH and promotion of healthy life styles though coordinated and inter-scrotal convergence approach.

A new scheme namely Janani Suraksha Yojana (JSY) under the umbrella scheme of NRHM has been introduced from April 2005 to enhance institutional delivery and reduce maternal mortality and morbidity among low economic strata. The scheme envisages the benefit of cash assistance with institutional care during delivery, preceded with antenatal care and immediate post partum care. This Program targets women living below poverty line who are of and above 19 years.

Another scheme namely, Vandemataram Scheme introduced by the Govt of India, across states intends to provide free antenatal and postnatal checkup, counseling on nutrition, breastfeeding, spacing of birth etc. through public private partnership. It also aims to reduce the maternal mortality and morbidity of the pregnant and expectant mothers by involving and utilizing the vast resources of specialists/trained workforce available in the private sector.

Under the National Plan of Action on Nutrition, the Ministry of Health and Family Welfare, Govt of India addresses the problem of nutritional anaemia among pregnant women and children. Adolescent girls are being increasingly recognised as a vulnerable group for anaemia. The National Nutrition Anaemia Control Programme is implemented through the primary healthcare infrastructure, with the female multipurpose health worker/ANM and other paramedical workers in health sub-centres and PHCs distributing iron folic acid (IFA) tablets. These tablets are available free of cost in all government health centres. Under the RCH project, each sub-centre receives 30,000 tablets of IFA every year as part of the drug kit A meant for the health sub-centre. The front line workers of the Integrated Child Development Services (ICDS) scheme also assist in distributing IFA tablets and dissemination of health education to mothers on prevention of anaemia.

The analysis done in the previous section was focused on three major issues. Firstly, the current status of maternal and child mortality, secondly plausible causes and thirdly pattern/coverage across various states on major strategies in place for addressing maternal and child health care in the country. The emerging trends show that there are marked variations across the States as for as health indicators are concerned.

3

REPRODUCTIVE HEALTH STATUS OF MARRIED ADOLESCENT GIRLS

Adolescents account for one fifth of the world's population and have been on an increasing trend. In India they account for 22.8% of the population. This implies that about 230 million Indians are adolescents in the age group of 10 to 19 years. The term adolescent means 'to emerge' or 'achieve identity'. Adolescence is defined as a phase of life characterized by rapid physical growth and development, physical, social and psychological changes and maturity, sexual maturity, experimentation, development of adult mental processes and a move from the earlier childhood socio-economic dependence towards relative independence. This is also the period of psychological transition from a child who has to live in a family to an adult who has to live in a society. Adolescents have very special and distinct needs, which can no longer be overlooked. It is also essential to invest in adolescents, as they are the future of the country. They need to be helped to help themselves and to be helped to do it alone. By addressing their needs one would not only be contributing to the socio-economic development of the country but also to other societal concerns like social harmony, gender justice, population stabilization and improving the quality of life. It has often been said that in India there is no phase such as 'adolescents'- from a child one becomes a young-adult.

Adolescents have often been viewed as a group of people with problems, disturbances and rebellion. However, the reality is somewhat different. Wherever positive stimulation and a congenial environment have been provided, adolescents have risen to the occasion and done proud. They yearn 'to right all wrongs', 'fight for justice" and 'do the right thing'. They are keen to be recognised as useful productive and participating citizens of society. Their contribution in the struggle for independence, the environment movement, national literacy campaign and campaigns against plastic bags and fire crackers are only some examples. However, where the right environment has not been provided they have taken to violence and have been drawn into petty and serious crime. Adolescents are imbibed with idealism, striving for justice and truth. The time has come for us, as a nation to seriously think about providing the right stimulus, role models and environment for adolescents, in order to become assets for nation building. They have the potential; now is the time to provide them with the opportunities.

Over the next two decades the number of adolescents as well as their share as a proportion to the total population will be large because of the high fertility in the eighties and the population momentum in the nineties. So far adolescents have not received the attention they deserve because of the relatively low morbidity and mortality rates of this age group. However, in view of the sheer numbers (230 million), adolescents as a group, merit special attention. Also, since adolescents comprise a major part of the reproductive age group, they will play a significant role in determining the future size and growth pattern of India's population.

DECLINING FEMALE-MALE RATIO

The ratio of females to males, according to the 2001 Census is 933:1000-a disturbing indicator of gender discrimination. State-wise sex ratios vary from 1058 in Kerala, 990 in Chhattisgarh, 861 in Haryana and 874 in Punjab. Out of the 12 million girls born in the country each year, 25 per cent or 3 million do not get to see their 15th birthday according to a UNICEF Report of

1995. The strong 'son preference' in India which manifests itself in the neglect and exploitation of girls and women has led to the adverse sex ratio. The sex ratio for adolescents in the 13-19 age groups declined from 897.7 in 1981 to 884.2 in 1991. There is also evidence to show that there is a high level of female mortality in the age group of 15 to 19 years implying high maternal mortality amongst teenage mothers. It will therefore be essential to consider the gender dimension in any plan for adolescents.

The results of the first population census of the millennium reveal a number of significant changes in the sex ratio patterns in the country. Firstly, the sex ratio decline among children in the age group 0-6 years turns out to be sharpening in the urban areas than the rural areas. Second, the traditional north-south divide stands significantly modified and the northernization of sex ratios is rapidly taking the urban route. The sharp decline in the urban female–male ratios among children can be explained away by three hatches of yesteryears i.e. migration, undercount or biologically ordained high sex ratios at birth. This decline points out to one factor, sex selective abortion or female foeticide that has gained currency during 1980 and more sharply in 1990's. Age wise sex ratio in India, as per 2001 census is shown in table 1. The decline in female male ratio during 1991-2001 in rural areas has been recorded higher in Punjab followed by Himachal Pradesh, Haryana, Delhi and Chandigarh. The decline of FMR during the corresponding period in urban areas has been reported highest in Punjab followed by Gujarat, Dadara Nagar Haveli, Haryana, Daman & Deu, Delhi, and Uttar Pradesh. Male female ratio in Uttar Pradesh during 1901 to 2001 has shown sharp variations. It has been reported quite low as compared to national average in all the census reports. (Table 1).

Sex ratio during 1901 to 2001 in various states is shown in table 2. There has been fluctuating trend in sex-ratio over the period. Overall the sex ratio has declined subsequently. The decline in sex ratio is more visible in Haryana, Punjab, Bihar, Uttar Pradesh, Tamil Nadu, Delhi, Mizoram, and Manipur. During 2001 Kerala, Pondicherry, Chhattisgarh, Tamil Nadu,

Manipur, Andhra Pradesh, Meghalaya, Orissa, Himachal Pradesh and Uttaranchal were placed among top 10 states where female male ratio was quite satisfactory.

Table 1
Female-Male Ratio during 1991-2001

State	*FMR Urban 2001*	*FMR Rural 2001*	*FMR Urban 1991*	*FMR Rural 1991*	*Decline Urban*	*Decline Rural*
India	903	934	935	948	32	14
Punjab	789	795	936	952	147	157
Gujarat	827	905	909	937	82	32
Haryana	809	824	884	877	75	53
Delhi	866	853	917	900	51	47
Uttar Pradesh	880	922	928	927	48	5
Himachal Pradesh	858	900	904	955	46	55
Uttaranchal	874	914	913	988	39	74
Chandigarh	844	852	879	891	35	39
Goa	919	948	953	972	34	24
Maharashtra	908	923	934	953	26	30
Bihar	924	940	950	953	26	13
Madhya Pradesh	906	941	931	944	25	3
Nagaland	935	983	959	1001	24	18
Assam	931	967	955	977	24	10
Orissa	927	954	949	969	22	15
Rajasthan	886	914	909	919	23	5
Chhattisgarh	941	982	960	988	19	6
Jharkhand	931	973	950	985	19	12
Sikkim	925	991	936	967	11	-24
Karnataka	939	954	951	963	12	9
Tripura	940	978	959	968	19	-10
West Bengal	948	967	955	969	7	2
Tamil Nadu	951	931	955	945	4	14

During 1981-90, ratio of males per 1000 females at birth was recorded high in Haryana, Punjab, Uttar Pradesh, Bihar, Gujarat, Rajasthan and Madhya Pradesh (Table 3).

Sex ratio in Uttaranchal during 1901-2001 is shown in table 4. The lowest sex ratio has been reported in Dehradun,

Hardwar, and Uttarkashi during 2001. Significantly, the sex ratio has declined sharply in Uttarkashi and Hardwar, while in a few districts; the sex ratio has increased gradually.

Table 2
Male Female Ratio in India

State	*1901*	*1911*	*1921*	*1931*	*1941*	*1951*	*1961*	*1971*	*1981*	*1991*	*2001*
India	972	964	955	950	945	946	841	930	933	927	933
Uttar Pradesh	937	915	909.	904	907	910	909	879	885	876	898
Bihar	1054	1044	1016	994.	966	990	994	954	946	907	921
Maharashtra	978	966	950	947	949	941	936	930	937	934	922
Andhra Pradesh	985	992	993	987	980	986	981	977	975	972	978
Tamil Nadu	1044	1042	1029	1027	1012	1007	992	978	977	974	986
West Bengal	945	9295	905	890	852	265	878	891	911	917	934
Madhya Pradesh	990	986	974	973	970	967	953	941	941	912	920
Karnataka	983	981	969	965	960	966	959	957	963	960	964
Gujarat	954	946	944	945	941.	952	940	934	942	934	921
Rajasthan	905	908	896	907	906	921	908	911	919	910	922
Orissa	1037	1056	1084	1067	1053	1022	1001	988	981	971	972
Kerala	1004	1008	1011	1022	1027	1028	1022	1016	1032	1036	1058
Punjab	832	780	799	815	836	844	854	865	879	882	874
Assam	919	915	896	874	875	868	869	896	901	923	932
Haryana	867	835	844	844	869	871	868	867	870	865	861
J & K	-	-	-	-	-	873	878	878	892	896	900
Himachal Pradesh	884	889	890	897	890	912	938	958	973	976	970
Delhi	862	793	733	722	715	768	785	801	808	827	821
Tripura	874	885	885	885	886	905	932	943	946	945	950
Goa	-	-	-	-	-	1128	1066	918	975	967	960
Manipur	1037	1029	1041	1065	1055	1036	1015	980	971	958	978
Arunachal	-	-	-	-	-	-	894	861	862	859	901
Nagaland	973	993	992	997	1021	999	933	871	863	886	909
Mizoram	1113	1120	1109	1102	1069	1041	1009	946	919	921	938
Uttaranchal	-	-	-	-	-	-	-	-	-	-	964
Chhattisgarh	-	-	-	-	-	-	-	-	-	-	990
Jharkhand	-	-	-	-	-	-	-	-	-	-	941
Sikkim	916	951	970	967	920	907	904	863	835	878	875

Source: RGI, Census of India 1991, Series 1, Total Population and Census 2001.

Table 3
Differences in sex ratio -Census 2001

State	*Female Male Ratio 2001*	*Place*	*Female Male Ratio (0-6 years)*	*Ratio of males per 1000 females at the time of birth 1981-90**
Kerala	1,058	1	962	1055
Pondichery	1001	2	958	-
Chhattisgarh	990	3	975	-
Tamil Nadu	986	4	939	1049
Manipur	978	5	961	-
Andhra Pradesh	978	6	964	1047
Meghalaya	975	7	975	-
Orissa	972	8	950	1062
Himachal Pradesh	970	9	897	-
Uttaranchal	964	10	906	-
Karnataka	964	11	949	1073
Goa	960	12	933	-
Tripura	950	13	975	-
Lakshadeep	947	14	974	-
Jharkhand	941	15	966	-
Mizoram	938	16	971	-
West Bengal	934	17	963	1056
India	933		927	1095
Assam	932	18	964	1064
Maharashtra	922	19	917	1085
Rajasthan	922	20	909	1141
Gujarat	921	21	878	1113
Bihar	921	22	938	1117
Madhya Pradesh	920	23	929	1082
Nagaland	909	24	975	-
Arunachal	901	25	961	-
J & K	900	26	937	-
Uttar Pradesh	898	27	916	1116
Sikkim	875	28	986	-
Punjab	874	29	793	1132
Haryana	861	30	820	1150
Andman Nikobar	846	31	965	-
Delhi	821	32	865	-
Dadara Nagar	811	33	973	-
Chandigarh	773	34	845	-
Daman Deev	709	35	925	-

Source: Registrar General of India.

Table 4
Uttaranchal Male/Female Sex Ratio 1901- 2001

State	*1901*	*1911*	*1921*	*1931*	*1941*	*1951*	*1961*	*1971*	*1981*	*1991*	*2001*
Uttarkashi	1015	1026	1035	1017	976	993	94	899	881	918	941
Chamoli	1028	1033	1080	1066	1073	1092	1103	1035	1020	982	1017
Rudraprayag	1061	1067	1105	1092	1084	1144	1169	1169	1121	1094	1117
Tehri	1006	1061	1025	1007	967	1122	1196	1179	1081	1048	1051
Dehradun	733	696	N.A.	N.A.	N.A.	N.A.	N.A.	N.A.	N.A.	843	893
Pauri	1031	1035	1083	1069	1076	1137	1163	1119	1091	1058	1104
Hardwar	864	823	818	820	802	806	796	803	817	846	868
Almora	989	983	1012	1011	1023	1060	1114	1100	1095	1099	1147
Bageshwar	936	931	959	957	969	1008	1024	1057	1031	1055	1110
Nainital	780	753	706	693	689	699	715	837	847	881	906
U.S. Nagar	812	785	737	723	720	731	726	774	841	863	902
Pithoragarh	977	971	1000	998	1010	1020	1052	1033	1027	992	1031
Champavat	928	924	946	947	961	956	929	955	947	945	1024
Uttaranchal	831	907	916	913	907	940	947	940	936	936	964

Source: Janganana Report-2001.

The sex ratio in Uttar Pradesh is shown in table 5. The sharp variations emerge in the regions and districts in the states. Western region has witnessed low sex ratio while eastern region has shown slightly better position. The sex ratio of children in the age group 0-6 years in Uttar Pradesh has declined, 11 points since 1991. Kanpur Nagar, Meerut, Sahjahanpur, Mujaffarnagar, Bagpat, Kanpur Dehat, Gautam Budh Nagar, Jalaun, Farrukhabad, Mathura, Auraiya, Aligarh, Hathras, Mainpuri, Ferozabad, and Etawah have witnessed low sex ratio whereas in backward areas like Sonbhadra, Maharajganj, Kushinagar, Gonda, Balrampur, Behraich and Sidharthnagar the child sex ratio is above 950.

Table 5
Sex Ratio since 1901 in Uttar Pradesh

Sl. No.	*State/District*	*Sex Ratio (Number of females per 1000 males)*										
		1901	*1911*	*1921*	*1931*	*1941*	*1951*	*1961*	*1971*	*1981*	*1991*	*2001*
1	2	3	4	5	6	7	8	9	10	11	12	13
	Uttar Pradesh	938	916	908	903	907	908	907	876	882	876	898
1.	Saharanpur	863	823	817	819	800	828	838	829	839	851	868
2.	Muzaffarnagar	869	817	829	828	825	826	841	831	843	860	872
3.	Bijnor	918	887	900	883	890	886	877	853	863	871	896

Sl. No.	*State/District*	*Sex Ratio (Number of females per 1000 males)*										
		1901	*1911*	*1921*	*1931*	*1941*	*1951*	*1961*	*1971*	*1981*	*1991*	*2001*
1	2	3	4	5	6	7	8	9	10	11	12	13
4.	Moradabad	882	861	869	860	862	859	858	834	840	849	885
5.	Rampur	897	876	866	855	845	863	871	836	843	858	882
6.	Jyotiba Phulenagar	906	885	893	884	886	883	881	845	849	860	885
7.	Meerut	874	844	847	835	845	826	839	830	841	858	871
8.	Baghpat	884	855	858	845	855	836	847	836	852	838	848
9.	Ghaziabad	877	852	854	841	853	854	847	830	840	840	860
10.	Gautam Buddha Nagar	893	882	882	868	889	874	871	848	909	817	842
11.	Bulandshahar	901	899	897	884	911	883	882'	855	865	858	881
12.	Aligarh	894	854	848	845	845	860	862	837	844	845	861
13.	Hathras	882	840	835	837	838	851	854	824	825	830	856
14.	Mathura	864	814	814	833	834	846	837	822	811	816	841
15.	Agra	864	833	818	830	848	847	842	829	828	832	852
16.	Firozabad	848	823	817	822	843	848	849	833	825	832	851
17.	Etah	851	838	847	845	847	870	865	833	827	824	847
18.	Mainpuri	837	817	816	817	840	865	858	831	833'	834	855
19.	Budaun	854	824	848	848	855	844	837	812	809	810	841
20.	Bareilly	862	843	861	849	846	844	834	817	830	839	872
21.	Pilibhit	884	861	884	864	861	858	842	827	846	853	876
22.	Shahjahanpur	862	841	852	836	822	826	826	797	813	816	838
23.	Kheri	891	875	883	872	869	850	853	824	846	842	875
24.	Sitapur	897	879	873	877	877	860	859	829	846	833	862
25.	Hardoi	876	839	850	853	861	864	857	825	827	818	843
26.	Unnao	957	903	889	890	896	902	892	88.9	889	873	898
27.	Lucknow	912	856	845	819	819	842	839	841	847	866	891
28.	Rae Bareli	1026	991	972	972	974	954	965	944	941	931	949
29.	Farrukhabad	853	826	831	831	873	842	832	810	817	832	860
30.	Kannauj	843	817	822	822	863	833	846	826	854	835	868
31.	Etawah	847	829	819	772	838	845	843	828	834	834	856
32.	Auraiya	837	819	809	849	828	835	853	824	827	828	856
33.	Kanpur Dehat	860	825	795	803	770	855	865	833	844	836	856
34.	Kanpur Nagar	871	836	806	813	781	770	788	803	825	832	869
35.	Jalaun	937	931	901	908	904	908	886	857	837	829	847
36.	Jhansi	956	946	924	932	935	916	890	879	869	864	870
37.	Lalitpur	956	946	924	932	935	931	905	855	858	863	884
38.	Hamirpur	985	975	956	950	950	935	923	879	853	839	852
39.	Mahoba	1011	999	979	965	973	947	925	877	861	845	866
40.	Banda	992	984	957	941	942	931	911	870	859	832	860

Contd...

Sl. No.	State/District	Sex Ratio (Number of females per 1000 males)										
		1901	1911	1921	1931	1941	1951	1961	1971	1981	1991	2001
1	2	3	4	5	6	7	8	9	10	11	12	13
41.	Chitrakoot	971	962	936	920	921	910	895	872	876	862	872
42.	Fatehpur	965	933	910	906	941	915	915	901	896	882	892
43.	Pratapgarh	1045	1057	1048	1049	965	1039	1062	1016	1006	987	983
44.	Kaushambi	1013	983	957	956	965	958	948	932	898	883	894
45.	Allahabad	997	968	942	941	950	943	924	889	888	873	882
46.	Barabanki	946	915.	912	911	901	889	885	845	780	854	886
47.	Faizabad	975	990	979	968	983	961	980	914 I	912	898	940
48.	Ambedkar Nagar	987	914	1000	984	996	973	980	932	962	943	977
49.	Sultanpur	1025	1030	1028	1023	1044	998	1017	970	971	933	980
50.	Bahraich	925	917	915	911	904	900	892	842	840	845	865
51.	Shrawasti	943	935	933	929	921	918	907	840	885	833	859
52.	Balrampur	964	965	956	954	944	931	917	867	883	868	896
53.	Gonda	965	966	957	954	945	936	942	881	908	877	899
54.	Siddhartnagar	974	976	955	947	943	965	950	908	924	912	946
55.	Basti	966	969	948	940	935	946	.936	887	917	908	916
56.	Sant Kabir Nagar	984	986	965	957	953	964	967	918	951	928	978
57.	Maharajganj	1011	995	974	955	981	964	963	916	919	909	933
58.	Gorakhpur	1011	995	974	955	981	996	985	925	952	924	959
59.	Kushinagar	983	967	938	917	940	975	969	931	955	940	961
60.	Deoria	1039	1023	993	971	995	1031	1036	986	1022	995	1003
61.	Azamgarh	1021	992	970	970	989	1024	1040	1006	1032	1007	1026
62.	Mau	1026	991	968	967	988	1001	1012	976	996	974	984
63.	Ballia	1085	996	949	947	986	1041	1037	975	984	946	952
64.	Jaunpur	1039	1008	1011	1017	1033	1024	1061	1011	1009	994	1021
65.	Ghazipur	1053	996	958	951	972	1000	1020	977	988	957	974
66.	Chandauli	1018	1011	982	974	'972	971	954	916	918	907	922
67.	Varanasi	968	961	934	925	924	923	915	886	890	890	908
68.	Bhadohi	1069	1062	1033	1024	1023	1022	1042	965	921	896	918
69.	Mirzapur	1045	1023	1003	999	1002	984	961	913	897	883	897
70.	Sonbhadra	1045	1023	1003	999	1002	967	900	887	874	862	896

Source: Census of India 2001: Uttar Pradesh, National Commission for Women, 2005.

Importantly, the highest number of ultrasound centres where sex determination of a foctus may be carried was reported in Agra. A study published in the Lancet, the British medical Journal, 2005 stated that over 10 million female foetuses may have been aborted in India in last 20 years. (Table 6).

Table 6
Sex Ratio and Ultrasound Centres in Uttar Pradesh

District		*Eastern UP*	
	Pop. Size (lakhs)	*U/S Centres*	*Sex Ratio*
Deoria	27.12	14	948
Kushinagar	28.93	10	955
Gorakhpur	37.69	79	934
Ghazipur	30.37	07	934
		Western UP	
Etah	27.90	15	891
Saharanpur	28.96	49	872
Agra	36.20	122	866
Badaun	30.69	14	890

AGE AT MARRIAGE

There is a large variation in child and adolescent marriages across the states. Rajasthan, Uttar Pradesh, Bihar and Madhya Pradesh have witnessed a large number of child and adolescent marriages while Kerala, Punjab have higher age at marriage. Moreover, 75 per cent of the total married women in the age group of 10-14 years come from large northern states of Bihar, Madhya Pradesh, Rajasthan and Uttar Pradesh. These few states also contribute as much as 51 per cent of the total married women in the next age group of 15-19 years. Moreover, social, economic and political forces are rapidly changing the ways that young people must prepare for adult life. These changes have enormous implications for adolescent's education, employment, marriage, childbearing and health. International attention on adolescent sexual activity tends to focus on premarital sex; however sexual debate among adolescent girls occurs largely within marriage. The sharp variations emerge among the states as a as average age at the birth of first child and last child is concerned. The average age at first child has been reported lowest in Andhra Pradesh, West Bengal, Tripura, Assam, Orissa, Karnataka and Bihar while highest age at first child has been reported in Goa, Mizoram, Manipur and Punjab.

Similarly, highest age at last child has been reported in Uttar Pradesh, Bihar, Rajasthan and Manipur (Table 7).

Table 7
Average Age at First and last Child

State	*Average age at the birth of first child*	*Average age at the birth of last child*	*Difference*
India	19.3	30.6	11.3
Uttar Pradesh	19.6	33.8	14.2
Bihar	18.8	32.7	13.9
Maharashtra	18.9	28.0	9.1
Andhra Pradesh	18.1	27.9	9.8
Tamil Nadu	19.3	29.1	9.8
West Bengal	18.2	29.8	11.6
Madhya Pradesh	18.9	31.1	12.2
Karnataka	18.8	29.2	10.4
Gujarat	20.0	29.3	9.3
Rajasthan	20.3	32.1	11.8
Orissa	18.8	30.9	12.1
Kerala	20.9	29.0	8.1
Punjab	21.4	30.0	8.6
Assam	18.4	31.8	13.4
Haryana	20.2	31.2	11.0
Himachal Pradesh	19.6	29.3	9.7
Delhi	20.1	29.6	9.6
J&K	19.6	31.1	11.5
Manipur	21.6	32.7	11.1
Meghalaya	20.8	31.5	10.7
Mizoram	22.0	31.8	9.8
Nagaland	21.1	30.1	9.0
Tripura	18.8	32.8	14.0
Goa	22.0	29.9	7.9

Source: International Institute of Population Science (1995), National Family Health Survey, India Pg. 118.

Nutrition is another very significant indicator of overall well-being and development of adolescent. This is explained by the fact that it is during this period that adolescents gain up to 50% of their adult weight, more than 20% of their adult height and 50% of their adult skeletal mass. Most of the current programmes of Government are focused either on pregnant and

Table 8
Institutional Delivery and Professional Assistance in Uttaranchal

No.	District	*Registration*		*Delivery at Institution*		*Delivery with health workers*		*Delivery with trained health attendants*		*Delivery without trained persons*		*Women with iron facilities*	
		2004	2003	2004	2003	2004	2003	2004	2003	2004	2003	2004	2003
1.	Dehradun	1816	2087	671	688	297	257	290	303	217	99	2054	1925
2.	Pauri	1059	1022	115	73	381	368	142	125	60	40	1054	1392
3.	Uttarkashi	524	537	76	58	108	108	79	101	15	35	411	370
4.	Tehri	1071	1113	55	35	309	310	164	180	49	18	986	-
5.	Chamoli	674	786	50	69	269	263	88	103	9	12	536	530
6.	Rudraprayag	448	482	56	40	187	151	91	86	17	13	261	299
7.	Hardwar	2902	3036	248	294	495	472	745	652	208	193	1699	1756
8.	Nainital	969	1258	220	158	322	288	281	509	45	18	1030	792
9.	U.S. Nagar	2612	2298	278	365	538	712	351	449	192	420	1330	1240
10.	Almora	749	616	44	27	270	214	82	50	73	50	395	408
11.	Bageshwar	416	467	65	19	231	236	27	34	38	39	126	170
12.	Pithoragarh	877	695	113	66	338	298	84	73	33	19	746	-
13.	Champavat	222	222	11	-	140	112	22	27	16	15	207	208
	Total	14339	14619	2002	1892	3879	3789	2446	2592	972	971	10835	9090

Source: National Commission for Women 2005.

lactating mothers or pre-school children. Adolescent nutrition has not been given the attention it deserves except for a limited nutrition programme for adolescent girls under the Integrated Child Development Services Scheme run by the Department of Women & Child Development. In fact it is during the spurt in growth during adolescence that mal-nutrition can be remedied -a fact little recognized even today.

In under-nourished children rapid growth during adolescence may increase the severity of under-nutrition. Iron is deficient in almost all age groups. Naturally the shortfalls create more vulnerability for adolescent girls. Pre-pregnancy anemic status of adolescent girls is crucial and has long-term inter-generational consequences. Anemic adolescent mothers are at a higher risk of miscarriages, maternal mortality and giving birth to still born, and low birth weight babies. 'Early marriage and pregnancy perpetuate both maternal and child under nutrition. In adolescents it also leads to poor academic performance in schools and low productivity in the work later.

A 1993 study reveals that in rural Rajasthan 93.3% of all girls suffered from first to third degree chronic energy deficiencies. The caloric intake of nutrients for' adolescent girls was deficient by 26 to 36%, with a 23 to 32% deficiency in protein. There is evidence to show that there has been an increase in obesity between 1975-79 and 1996-97 among adolescents especially among affluent groups both in rural and urban areas. There is therefore a need to combat both under -nutrition and over-nutrition.

There is also a high co-relation between the age at marriage" fertility management and family health with education levels. While the age at marriage for illiterate females is 15 years, it is 22 years for women who have completed school education. Thirty per cent of adolescents in the age group of 15 to 19 years are married, and in the age group of 25 to 29 years, 94 per cent were married. The age at marriage is about two and half years lower in rural areas compared to urban areas. The median age at first birth for women (20 to 49 years) is 19.6. The percentage of adolescents married before they are 18 is 68.3% in Rajasthan, and 71% in Bihar as against 170/0 in Kerala and 11.60/0 in

Punjab. In India, most fertility occurs within marriage and this makes the age at marriage of paramount importance for fertility rates. According to NFHS I (1992-93) 36% of married adolescents in the age group of 13 to 16 are already mothers or are pregnant with their first child as are 64% of those in the 17 to 19 years age group. Age specific fertility rates are given in a time series in the table below.

Table 9
India: Age Specific Fertility Rates

Age Group	*1980*	*1990*	*1992*	*1993*	*1995*
15-19	88.2	83.1	74.4	69.6	55.2
20-24	246.1	237.0	235.2	234.4	238.4

Source: CSO, Women and Men in India 1998.

Adolescent fertility varies greatly between states. In the age group of 13 to 19 years, adolescent fertility is 153 births per 1000 in Madhya Pradesh, 143 in Haryana, 141 in Maharashtra, and as low as 38 in Kerala. While knowledge about family planning is becoming widespread, availability of services seems to be lacking. Sixteen per cent of currently married women in India have an unmet need for family planning, implying that though they do not want any more children for at least two years, they are not using any contraception. The unmet need is highest in the age group of 15 to 19 years.

Adolescents are generally considered to be a healthy group and their mortality rates are lower than rates for other age groups. The table below reveals this amply. However the male female differentials, in mortality rates are very noticeable. This is probably due to the lower nutritional status of girls, early marriage and high adolescent fertility.

NFHS-II revealed that in many ways reproductive health of married adolescent women needs to be improved. However, a single uniform strategy across India would not be successful, owing to extreme inter state variation in reproductive health, average age at marriage, contraceptive use and decision making. Strict implementation of the law regarding legal minimum age at marriage as well as IEC activities to create awareness about reproductive health issues and to change attitudes are crucial to resolve the emergent problems. The NFHS-II findings generally emphasize the considerable risk that adolescents continue to face, extending from unsafe or unwanted sexual activities to such consequences as unwanted pregnancy, abortion and infection, and from misperceptions to *lack of life* skills and wide gender power imbalances. They also *under score* the vast obstacles that must be overcome in order to access contraceptives and other reproductive health, information and services.

Table 10
Age - Specific Mortality Rates

Age group	*1980*		*1990*		*1995*	
	Female	*Male*	*Female*	*Male*	*Female*	*Male*
0-4 years	43.5	40.1	27.9	24.8	25.3	23.2
4-9 years	4	3.3	2.8	2.3	2.7	2.2
1 0-14 years	1.7	1.7	1.4	1.4	1.4	1.3
15-19 years	2.9	2	0.5	1.7	2	1.7
20-24 years	3.8	2.3	3.1	2.4	2.7	2.1
All ages	12.4	12.4	9.6	9.7	8.7	9.3

Source: Central Statistical Organization, 1999: Women & Men in India 1998.

4

PROFILE OF RESPONDENTS

It has been already mentioned that 600 women were surveyed to examine their health status and their access to public health services. In this part of the report, an attempt has been made to analyse their socio-economic status and family background.

BACKGROUND OF RESPONDENTS

Age wise distribution of respondents is shown in table 1. Most of the women were belonging to the middle age group i.e. 26-45 years. There are sharp variations across the districts and states as far as age group of respondents is concerned.

Education of respondents is given in table 2. About one third respondents were found to -be either illiterate or literate only. The proportion of illiteracy is more pronounced in Uttar Pradesh as compared to Uttaranchal. Again, educational levels were reported higher in Uttaranchal. About 19 per cent respondents were graduate and above. It was reported as high as 22.33 per cent in Uttaranchal as compared to Uttar Pradesh (15 per cent).

Religion of respondents is shown in table 3. The overwhelming majority of the respondents are found to be Hindus (89.83) per cent). Their proportion has been recorded slightly higher in Uttar Pradesh as compared to Uttaranchal. Interestingly, the proportion of Muslim respondents has been

Table 1
Age Group of Respondents

	Uttar Pradesh				Uttaranchal				Total
	Azamgarh	*Jhansi*	*Sitapur*	*Sub-total*	*Dehradun*	*Pithora-garh*	*Udham Singh Nagar*	*Sub-total*	
Less then 18 years	3 [3.00]	5 [4.50]	2 [2.20]	10 [3.30]	6 [5.21]	8 [8.42]	10 [11.11]	24 [8.00]	34 [5.60]
19-25 years	20 [20.00]	24 [21.80]	28 [31.11]	72 [24.00]	21 [18.26]	20 [21.05]	15 [16.66]	56 [18.66]	128 [21.30]
26-35 years	30 [30.00]	29 [26.36]	18 [20.00]	77 [25.66]	32 [21.82]	19 [20.00]	26 [28.88]	77 [25.66]	154 [25.66]
36-45 years	25 [25.00]	27 [24.50]	21 [23.30]	73 [24.33]	24 [20.86]	22 [23.15]	18 [20.00]	64 [21.33]	137 [22.80]
46-55 years	7 [7.00]	10 [9.09]	8 [8.80]	25 [8.33]	25 [21.73]	14 [14.73]	15 [16.66]	54 [18.00]	79 [13.16]
55 to above	15 [15.00]	15 [13.60]	13 [14.40]	43 [14.33]	7 [6.08]	12 [12.63]	6 [6.66]	25 [8.33]	68 [11.33]
N	100	110	90	300	115	95	90	300	600

Table 2
Education of Respondents

	Uttar Pradesh				Uttaranchal				Total
	Azamgarh	*Jhansi*	*Sitapur*	*Sub-total*	*Dehradun*	*Pithora-garh*	*Udham Singh Nagar*	*Sub-total*	
Illiterate	18 [18.00]	21 [19.09]	15 [16.66]	54 [18.00]	13 [11.30]	18 [18.94]	11 [12.2]	42 [14.00]	96 [16.00]
Literate	9 [9.00]	26 [23.63]	13 [14.44]	48 [16.00]	10 [8.69]	21 [22.10]	9 [10.00]	40 [13.33]	88 [14.60]
Up to Primary	11 [11.00]	19 [17.27]	10 [11.11]	40 [13.33]	13 [11.30]	12 [12.63]	14 [15.55]	39 [13.00]	79 [13.16]
Jr. High School	18 [18.00]	18 [16.36]	20 [22.22]	56 [18.60]	25 [21.73]	13 [13.68]	12 [13.33]	50 [16.66]	106 [17.60]
Intermediate	21 [21.00]	12 [10.30]	18 [20.00]	51 [17.00]	20 [17.39]	10 [10.52]	25 [27.77]	55 [18.33]	106 [17.60]
Graduate	14 [14.00]	7 [6.36]	9 [10.00]	30 [10.00]	21 [18.26]	11 [11.57]	10 [11.11]	42 [14.00]	72 [12.00]
Post Graduate	7 [7.00]	6 [2.72]	5 [5.55]	15 [5.00]	10 [8.69]	6 [6.31]	9 [10.00]	25 [8.33]	40 [6.60]
Others	2 [2.00]	4 [3.63]	-	6 [2.00]	3 [2.60]	4 [4.21]	-	7 [2.10]	13 [2.16]
N	100	110	90	300	115	95	90	300	600

Table 3
Religion of Respondents

	Uttar Pradesh				Uttaranchal				Total
	Azamgarh	*Jhansi*	*Sitapur*	*Sub-total*	*Dehradun*	*Pithora-garh*	*Udham Singh Nagar*	*Sub-total*	
Hindu	97 [97.00]	101 [91.81]	83 [92.22]	281 [93.66]	108 [93.91]	92 [96.84]	58 [64.44]	258 [68.00]	539 [89.83]
Christian	-	-	-	-	-	-	2 [2.22]	2 [0.66]	2 [0.33]
Muslim	3 [3.00]	9 [8.18]	7 [7.77]	19 [6.33]	7 [6.08]	-	-	7 [2.33]	26 [4.33]
Sikh	-	-	-	-	-	-	30 [33.33]	30 [10.00]	30 [5.00]
Jain	-	-	-	-	-	-	-	-	-
Other	-	-	-	-	-	3 [3.15]	-	3 [1.00]	3 [0.50]
N	100	110	90	300	115	95	90	300	600

Table 4
Caste of Respondents

	Uttar Pradesh				Uttaranchal				Total
	Azamgarh	*Jhansi*	*Sitapur*	*Sub-total*	*Dehradun*	*Pithora-garh*	*Udham Singh Nagar*	*Sub-total*	
General	29 [29.00]	-	19 [21.11]	48 [16.00]	52 [45.21]	59 [62.10]	31 [34.44]	142 [47.33]	190 [31.66]
OBC	51 [51.00]	60 [54.54]	52 [57.77]	163 [54.33]	48 [41.73]	26 [27.36]	12 [13.33]	86 [28.66]	249 [41.50]
SC	15 [15.00]	41 [37.27]	12 [13.33]	68 [22.66]	8 [6.95]	7 [7.36]	10 [11.11]	25 [8.33]	93 [15.50]
ST	2 [2.00]	-	-	2 [0.66]	-	-	5 [5.55]	5 [1.66]	7 [1.16]
Muslim	3 [3.00]	9 [8.18]	7 [7.77]	19 [6.33]	7 [6.08]	-	-	7 [2.33]	26 [4.33]
Other	-	-	-	-	-	3 [3.15]	32 [35.55]	35 [11.66]	35 [5.83]
N	100	110	90	300	115	95	90	300	600

reported to be high in Jhansi followed by Sitapur in Uttar Pradesh.

About one third respondents were from general castes. It was found more pronouncing in Pithoragarh (62.10 per cent) followed by Dehradun (45.21 per cent) in Uttaranchal. has been recorded as low as 16 per cent in Uttar Pradesh. More than half of the respondents in Uttar Pradesh were belonging to backward castes while about one fourth women were belonging to scheduled castes and scheduled tribes. The proportion of scheduled castes and scheduled tribes has been found very low in Uttaranchal (Table 4).

Annual income of respondent's family is shown in table 5. The average income per family has been computed to be Rs. 59124.00 while it was recorded much higher in Udhamsingh Nagar ie. Rs. 72575.00. The lowest per household income has been reported to be in Jhansi i.e. Rs. 40275.00. Most of the respondents were found belonging to income level of Rs. 25000.00–7500.00 Only 10 per cent women had household income above Rs. 100000.00. This was recorded comparatively higher in Uttaranchal as compared to Uttar Pradesh.

Main occupation of respondents is given in table 6. Most of the surveyed women reported that their main occupation is agriculture. However, they are housewives as well. A large number of women were also reported as labourers and were engaged in petty business. The proportion of service class women has been reported to be higher in Dehradun and Pithoragarh districts. About one fourth respondents revealed that they have migrated. It was found more pronouncing in Udhamsingh Nagar and Jhansi districts. Those migrated belonged to rural areas (60.0 per cent).

The rural to urban migration has been reported to be higher in Uttar Pradesh (89.18 per cent) as compared to Uttaranchal (34.52 per cent). More than one third respondents in Udhamsingh Nagar also reported that they have migrated form small districts (Table 7).

Caste wise migration level is shown in table 8. In the state of Uttar Pradesh, migration level is more pronounced among OBC's, and scheduled castes respondents while it was recorded

Table 5
Annual Income of Respondents

	Uttar Pradesh				*Uttaranchal*				*Total*
	Azamgarh	*Jhansi*	*Sitapur*	*Sub-total*	*Dehradun*	*Pithora-garh*	*Udham Singh Nagar*	*Sub-total*	
Less then 25000	28 [28.00]	42 [38.18]	9 [10.00]	79 [26.33]	12 [10.43]	26 [27.36]	5 [5.55]	43 [14.33]	122 [20.33]
25000-50000	29 [29.00]	26 [23.63]	21 [23.33]	76 [25.33]	20 [17.39]	38 [40.00]	18 [20.00]	76 [25.33]	152 [25.33]
50000-75000	32 [32.00]	30 [27.27]	10 [11.11]	72 [24.00]	40 [34.78]	17 [17.89]	6 [6.66]	63 [21.00]	135 [22.50]
75000-100000	9 [9.00]	12 [10.90]	40 [44.44]	61 [20.33]	33 [28.69]	11 [11.57]	25 [27.77]	69 [23.00]	130 [21.66]
More then 100000	2 [2.00]	-	10 [11.11]	12 [4.00]	10 [8.69]	3 [3.15]	36 [40.00]	49 [16.33]	61 [10.16]
N	100	110	90	300	115	95	90	300	600
Average Annual Income	52350	40225	70500	54358	76500	42600	72575	63891	59124

Table 6
Main Occupation of Respondents

	Uttar Pradesh				*Uttaranchal*				*Total*
	Azamgarh	*Jhansi*	*Sitapur*	*Sub-total*	*Dehradun*	*Pithora-garh*	*Udham Singh Nagar*	*Sub-total*	
Agriculture	80 [80.00]	32 [29.09]	68 [75.55]	180 [60.00]	-	29 [30.52]	51 [56.66]	80 [26.66]	260 [43.33]
Business	5 [5.00]	-	3 [3.33]	8 [2.66]	8 [6.95]	24 [25.26]	27 [30.00]	59 [19.66]	67 [11.16]
Service	6 [6.00]	2 [1.81]	4 [4.44]	12 [4.00]	42 [36.52]	32 [33.68]	12 [13.33]	86 [28.66]	98 [16.33]
Labour	9 [9.00]	74 [67.27]	13 [14.44]	96 [32.00]	24 [20.86]	10 [10.52]	-	34 [11.33]	130 [21.66]
Others	-	2 [1.81]	2 [2.22]	4 [1.33]	41 [35.62]	-	-	41 [13.66]	45 [7.50]
N	100	110	90	300	115	95	90	300	600

Table 7
Whether Migrated

	Uttar Pradesh				*Uttaranchal*				*Total*
	Azamgarh	*Jhansi*	*Sitapur*	*Sub-total*	*Dehradun*	*Pithora-garh*	*Udham Singh Nagar*	*Sub-total*	
Yes	16 [16.00]	46 [41.81]	12 [10.90]	64 [21.33]	24 [20.86]	11 [11.57]	49 [54.44]	84 [28.00]	148 [24.67]
No	84 [84.00]	64 [58.18]	78 [70.90]	236 [78.66]	91 [79.13]	84 [88.42]	41 [45.55]	216 [72.00]	452 [75.33]
N	100	110	90	300	115	95	90	300	600
If yes									
Rural	10 [62.50]	46 [100.00]	10 [83.33]	56 [87.50]	14 [58.33]	4 [36.36]	11 [22.44]	29 [34.52]	95 [60.12]
Small District	6 [37.50]	-	2 [16.66]	8 [95.2]	2 [8.33]	7 [63.63]	18 [36.73]	27 [32.14]	35 [22.15]
Other State	-	-	-	-	8 [33.33]	-	20 [40.81]	28 [33.33]	28 [17.72]
Other Country	-	-	-	-	-	-	-	-	-
N	16	46	12	64	24	11	49	84	158

high among general castes in Uttaranchal state. About two fifth respondents belonging to general castes have migrated. It is because of the fact that Uttaranchal state comprises of quite little proportion of OBC's population.

Table 8
Caste wise Migration of Respondents

	Uttar Pradesh			*Uttaranchal*		
	Migration			*Migration*		
	Yes	*No*	*Sub-total*	*Yes*	*No*	*Sub-total*
General	7 [10.94]	41 [17.37]	48 [16.00]	36 [42.86]	106 [49.07]	142 [47.33]
OBC	38 [59.38]	125 [52.97]	136 [54.33]	20 [23.81]	66 [30.56]	86 [28.67]
SC	15 [23.44]	53 [22.46]	68 [22.67]	13 [15.48]	12 [5.56]	25 [8.33]
ST	2 [3.13]	-	2 [66.67]	5 [10.42]	-	5 [1.67]
Muslim	2 [3.13]	17 [7.20]	19 [6.33]	2 [2.38]	5 [2.31]	7 [2.33]
Others	-	-	-	8 [9.52]	27 [12.50]	35 [11.67]
N	64	236	300	84	216	300

Occupation wise migration level of respondents is shown in table 9. In the state of Uttar Pradesh, about 38 per cent migrated respondents were found to be labourers while in the state of Uttaranchal, 29 per cent respondents belonging to labour class have migrated. Thus, it is clear that migration level is more pronounced among wage earners, and labour class.

Table 9
Main Occupation of Migrated Respondents

	Uttar Pradesh			*Uttaranchal*		
	Migration			*Migration*		
	Yes	*No*	*Sub-total*	*Yes*	*No*	*Sub-total*
Agriculture	5 [7.81]	175 [74.15]	180 [60.00]	18 [21.43]	62 [28.70]	80 [26.67]
Business	-	8 [3.39]	8 [2.67]	18 [21.43]	41 [18.98]	59 [19.67]
Service	3 [4.69]	9 [3.81]	12 [4.00]	15 [17.86]	71 [32.87]	86 [28.67]
Labour	56 [87.50]	40 [16.95]	96 [32.00]	24 [28.57]	10 [4.63]	34 [11.33]
Others	-	4 [1.69]	4 [1.33]	9 [10.71]	32 [14.81]	41 [13.67]
N	64	236	300	84	216	300

Table 10
Age Group of Household

	Uttar Pradesh				Uttaranchal				Total
	Azamgarh	*Jhansi*	*Sitapur*	*Sub-total*	*Dehradun*	*Pithora-garh*	*Udham Singh Nagar*	*Sub-total*	
Less then 10 years	112 [22.36]	136 [25.76]	92 [20.22]	340 [22.91]	112 [24.35]	70 [15.95]	100 [22.12]	282 [20.87]	622 [21.94]
11-18 years	115 [22.95]	73 [13.82]	86 [18.90]	274 [18.46]	55 [11.96]	135 [30.75]	95 [21.02]	285 [21.10]	559 [19.72]
19-25 years	50 [9.98]	67 [12.68]	84 [18.46]	201 [13.54]	85 [18.48]	16 [3.64]	86 [19.03]	187 [13.84]	388 [13.69]
26-35 years	66 [13.17]	105 [19.89]	88 [19.34]	259 [17.45]	76 [16.52]	31 [7.06]	35 [7.74]	142 [10.51]	401 [14.14]
36-45 years	111 [22.16]	58 [10.98]	99 [21.76]	268 [18.06]	33 [7.17]	123 [28.02]	40 [8.85]	196 [14.51]	464 [16.37]
46-55 years	23 [4.59]	58 [10.98]	6 [1.32]	87 [5.86]	48 [10.43]	13 [2.96]	51 [11.28]	112 [8.29]	199 [7.02]
55 to above	24 [4.79]	31 [5.87]	-	55 [3.71]	51 [11.09]	51 [11.62]	45 [9.96]	147 [10.88]	202 [7.25]
N	501	528	455	1484	460	439	452	1351	2835
Family Size	5.01	4.8	5.05	5.95	4.0	4.62	5.02	4.50	4.72

Table 11
Sex of Household Population

	Uttar Pradesh				Uttaranchal				Total
	Azamgarh	*Jhansi*	*Sitapur*	*Sub-total*	*Dehradun*	*Pithora-garh*	*Udham Singh Nagar*	*Sub-total*	
Male	239 [47.70]	305 [57.77]	255 [56.04]	799 [53.84]	288 [62.61]	228 [51.94]	248 [54.87]	764 [56.55]	1563 [55.13]
Female	262 [52.30]	223 [42.23]	200 [43.96]	685 [46.13]	172 [37.39]	211 [48.06]	204 [45.13]	587 [43.45]	1272 [44.87]
N	501	528	455	1484	460	439	452	1351	2835
Sex Ratio	1096	731	784	857	597	925	822	768	814

FAMILY BACKGROUND

An attempt has been made here to analyse the family background of respondents. Age group of household population is shown in table 10. The average family size has been reported to be 4.72 members. The size of family has been reported to be larger in Uttar Pradesh as compared to Uttaranchal. More than two fifth populations comprises of children (upto 18 years). Most of the household population is belonging to middle age groups i.e. 19-45 years. The proportion of adolescents has been reported significantly high in Uttaranchal as compared to Uttar Pradesh. The proportion of population above 55 years constituted 7.25 per cent, comparatively higher in Uttaranchal.

Gender-wise distribution of household population is shown in table 11. Out of total population, 55.13 per cent population comprises of males. This proportion was reported to be significantly higher in Dehradun (62.61 per cent) followed by Jhansi (57.77 per cent) and lowest in Azamgarh (47.70 per cent). Thus, sex ratio has been recorded significantly higher in Azamgarh followed by Pithoragarh and Udhamsingh Nagar.

Table 12
Gender wise Age Distribution of Household

	Uttar Pradesh			*Uttaranchal*			*Total*
	Male	*Female*	*Sex Ratio*	*Male*	*Female*	*Sex Ratio*	*Sex-Ratio*
Less then 10 years	185	155	838	161	121	752	798
11-18 years	145	129	890	155	130	828	863
19-25 years	106	95	896	107	80	748	822
26-35 years	137	122	890	82	60	731	831
36-45 years	148	120	811	111	85	766	792
46-55 years	48	39	813	62	50	806	809
55 to above	30	25	833	86	61	709	741
N	799	685	857	764	587	768	814

Gender-wise age group of household population is given in table 12. Sex ratio has been recorded significantly adverse in the low age group i.e. less than 18 years while in the higher age groups, the sex ratio is higher. Thus, the ratio of girls to boys is

Table 13
Education of Household Population

	Uttar Pradesh				Uttaranchal				Total
	Azamgarh	*Jhansi*	*Sitapur*	*Sub-total*	*Dehradun*	*Pithora-garh*	*Udham Singh Nagar*	*Sub-total*	
Illiterate	76 [15.17]	112 [21.21]	32 [7.03]	220 [14.82]	59 [12.83]	39 [8.88]	40 [8.85]	138 [10.21]	358 [12.63]
Literate	72 [14.37]	62 [11.74]	46 [10.11]	180 [12.13]	41 [8.91]	89 [20.27]	80 [17.70]	210 [15.54]	390 [13.76]
Up to Primary	113 [22.55]	113 [21.40]	100 [21.98]	326 [21.97]	42 [9.13]	55 [12.53]	60 [13.27]	157 [11.62]	483 [17.04]
Jr. High School	78 [15.57]	120 [22.73]	101 [22.20]	299 [20.15]	87 [18.91]	81 [18.45]	73 [16.15]	241 [17.84]	540 [19.05]
Intermediate	52 [10.38]	55 [10.42]	87 [19.72]	194 [13.07]	55 [11.96]	63 [14.35]	65 [14.38]	183 [13.55]	377 [13.30]
Graduate	30 [5.99]	13 [2.46]	35 [7.69]	78 [5.26]	64 [13.91]	59 [13.44]	59 [13.05]	182 [13.47]	260 [9.17]
Post Graduate	23 [4.59]	3 [0.57]	18 [3.96]	44 [2.96]	32 [6.96]	29 [6.61]	46 [10.18]	107 [7.92]	151 [5.33]
Others	57 [11.38]	50 [9.47]	36 [7.91]	143 [9.64]	80 [17.39]	24 [5.47]	29 [6.42]	133 [9.84]	276 [9.74]
N	501	528	455	1484	460	439	452	1351	2835

Table 14
Main Activity of Household Population

	Uttar Pradesh				Uttaranchal				Total
	Azamgarh	*Jhansi*	*Sitapur*	*Sub-total*	*Dehradun*	*Pithora-garh*	*Udham Singh Nagar*	*Sub-total*	
Child	114 [22.75]	96 [18.18]	128 [28.13]	338 [22.78]	87 [18.91]	103 [23.46]	95 [21.02]	285 [21.10]	623 [21.98]
Housewife	100 [19.96]	65 [12.31]	99 [21.76]	264 [17.79]	83 [18.04]	71 [16.17]	68 [15.04]	222 [16.43]	486 [17.14]
Working	84 [16.77]	198 [37.50]	108 [23.74]	390 [26.28]	139 [30.22]	126 [28.70]	128 [28.32]	393 [29.09]	783 [27.62]
Aged	76 [15.17]	39 [7.39]	14 [3.08]	129 [8.69]	49 [10.65]	49 [11.16]	20 [4.42]	118 [8.73]	247 [8.71]
Unemployed	75 [14.97]	80 [15.15]	55 [12.09]	210 [14.15]	39 [8.48]	48 [10.93]	65 [14.38]	152 [11.25]	362 [12.77]
Others	52 [10.38]	50 [9.47]	51 [11.21]	153 [10.31]	63 [13.70]	42 [9.57]	76 [16.81]	181 [13.40]	334 [11.78]
N	501	528	455	1484	460	439	452	1351	2835

found to be low, which is a negative trend and calls for serious attention.

Education of household population is shown in table 13. About one fourth household population is found to be either illiterate or a little literate only. About 15 per cent population had higher educational levels. Educational levels were reported significantly higher in Uttaranchal as compared to Uttar Pradesh. Despite the tough terrain and poor supply of education development facilities/infrastructure, the educational levels in Uttaranchal are higher.

Main activity of household population is given in table 14. About 22 per cent household population comprises of children. This proportion is found to be higher in Sitapur district as compared to other districts. About 17 per cent household population comprises of housewives. This was found more pronouncing in Sitapur district. More than one fourth population is reported to be working. The proportion of working population has been recorded higher in Jhansi (37.50 per cent), Dehradun (30.22 per cent) and low in Azamgarh (16.77 per cent) district. About 9 per cent of household population is of aged. This is reported higher in Azamgarh (15.17 per cent), Pithoragarh (11.16 per cent) and Dehradun (10.65 per cent). About 13 per cent population comprises of unemployed youths. It is reported high in Jhansi and Udhamsingh Nagar.

Marital status of household population is shown in table 15. About half of the population has been reported to be married while less than one third is found to be unmarried. The proportion of widows and separated has been reported to be high i.e. about 13 per cent. The proportion of widows has been recorded to be high in Uttaranchal as compared to Uttar Pradesh.

Occupation of household population is shown in table 16. Agriculture and agriculture labour constitute a major share in economy. However, services sector is found to be significant in the surveyed areas since about 15 per cent household population comprises of pervice class. It class has been recorded higher in Uttaranchal as compared to Uttar Pradesh.

Table 15
Marital Status of Household Population

	Uttar Pradesh				Uttaranchal				Total
	Azamgarh	*Jhansi*	*Sitapur*	*Sub-total*	*Dehradun*	*Pithora-garh*	*Udham Singh Nagar*	*Sub-total*	
Married	269 [53.69]	282 [53.41]	223 [49.01]	774 [52.16]	202 [43.91]	218 [49.66]	206 [45.58]	626 [46.34]	1400 [49.38]
Unmarried	157 [31.34]	139 [26.33]	171 [37.58]	467 [31.47]	145 [31.52]	135 [30.75]	142 [31.42]	422 [31.24]	889 [31.36]
Divorced	30 [5.99]	20 [3.79]	15 [3.30]	65 [4.38]	47 [10.22]	32 [7.29]	36 [7.96]	115 [8.51]	180 [6.35]
Separated	17 [3.39]	59 [11.17]	16 [3.52]	92 [6.20]	35 [7.61]	23 [5.24]	40 [8.85]	98 [7.25]	190 [6.70]
Widow	28 [5.59]	28 [5.30]	30 [6.59]	86 [5.80]	31 [6.74]	31 [7.06]	28 [6.19]	90 [6.66]	176 [6.21]
Others	-	-	-	-	-	-	-	-	-
N	501	528	455	1484	460	439	452	1351	2835

Table 16
Occupation of Household Population

	Uttar Pradesh				Uttaranchal				Total
	Azamgarh	*Jhansi*	*Sitapur*	*Sub-total*	*Dehradun*	*Pithora-garh*	*Udham Singh Nagar*	*Sub-total*	
Agriculture	153 [30.54]	119 [22.54]	126 [27.69]	398 [26.82]	83 [18.04]	105 [23.92]	110 [24.34]	298 [22.06]	696 [24.55]
Agriculture Labour	80 [15.97]	70 [13.26]	80 [17.58]	230 [15.50]	84 [18.26]	86 [19.59]	85 [18.81]	255 [18.87]	485 [14.11]
Labour	83 [16.57]	75 [14.20]	43 [9.45]	201 [13.54]	65 [14.13]	42 [9.57]	56 [12.39]	163 [12.07]	364 [12.84]
Service	45 [8.98]	95 [17.99]	80 [17.58]	220 [14.82]	100 [21.74]	56 [12.76]	60 [13.27]	216 [15.99]	436 [15.38]
Business	25 [4.99]	45 [8.52]	25 [4.40]	95 [6.40]	21 [4.57]	47 [10.71]	54 [11.95]	122 [9.03]	217 [7.66]
Others	115 [22.95]	124 [23.48]	101 [22.20]	340 [22.91]	107 [23.26]	103 [23.46]	87 [19.25]	297 [21.98]	637 [22.47]
N	501	528	455	1484	460	439	452	1351	2835

Housing conditions of surveyed areas are analysed to understand the living conditions, sanitation and hygienic conditions of the dwellers. More than half of the respondents said that they are living in pacca houses. It was found more pronouncing in Udhamsingh Nagar (66.66 per cent) and Dehradun (61.73 per cent). Only 36.36 per cent respondents in Jhansi were found living in pacca houses. 17 per cent respondents reported that they are living in mixed houses i.e. kachcha and pacca houses. The proportion of thatched houses has been reported significantly higher in Pithoragarh (8.42 per cent). Housing conditions are better placed in Uttaranchal as compared to Uttar Pradesh (Table 17).

Type of toilet is shown in table 18. More than one third respondents accepted that they have flush toilets. This was found more pronouncing in Dehradun and Udhamsingh Nagar. Importantly, 54 per cent respondents in Uttaranchal said that they have flush toilets as against 14.33 per cent in Uttar Pradesh. About 14 per cent respondents revealed that they have service toilets which need manual scavenging. These were found more pronouncing in Udhamsingh Nagar (31.11 per cent) followed by Pithoragarh (25.36 per cent).

Sources of drinking water are shown in table 19. About one third respondents reported that they are fetching drinking water from tap. It was reported very high i.e. 97.39 per cent in Dehradun. Uttar Pradesh is found to be backward in terms of sole drinking water. Most of the respondents in Uttar Pradesh get drinking water from hand pump. Unsafe sources of drinking water was found significantly larger in Jhansi (25.44 per cent) and Pithoragarh (47.36 per cent).

Type of cooking devices is shown in table 20. About half of the respondents accepted that they use Mud chullah for cooking of food. This proportion has been reported significantly high in Uttar Pradesh (69.33 per cent) as compared to Uttaranchal (29.66 per cent). About one third respondents accepted that they use gas as cooking device. This was found more pronouncing in Dehradun and Pithoragarh districts.

The respondents were asked regarding electrification of their houses. About half of the respondents said that their houses

Table 17
Type of Houses

	Uttar Pradesh				Uttaranchal				Total
	Azamgarh	*Jhansi*	*Sitapur*	*Sub-total*	*Dehradun*	*Pithora-garh*	*Udham Singh Nagar*	*Sub-total*	
Pacca	47 [47.00]	40 [36.36]	48 [53.33]	135 [45.00]	71 [61.73]	40 [42.10]	60 [66.66]	171 [57.00]	306 [51.00]
Kachcha	38 [38.00]	34 [30.90]	22 [24.44]	94 [31.33]	35 [30.43]	30 [31.57]	17 [18.88]	82 [27.33]	176 [29.33]
Thatched	-	5 [4.54]	3 [3.33]	8 [2.66]	-	8 [8.42]	-	8 [2.66]	16 [2.66]
Mixed	15 [15.00]	31 [28.18]	17 [18.88]	63 [21.00]	9 [7.82]	17 [17.89]	13 [14.44]	39 [13.00]	102 [17.00]
Others	-	-	-	-	-	-	-	-	-
N	100	110	90	300	115	95	90	300	600

Table 18
Type of Toilet

	Uttar Pradesh				Uttaranchal				Total
	Azamgarh	*Jhansi*	*Sitapur*	*Sub-total*	*Dehradun*	*Pithora-garh*	*Udham Singh Nagar*	*Sub-total*	
Flush	9 [9.00]	21 [19.09]	13 [14.44]	43 [14.33]	68 [59.13]	44 [46.31]	50 [55.55]	162 [54.00]	205 [34.16]
Service	3 [3.00]	3 [2.72]	8 [8.88]	14 [4.66]	17 [14.78]	24 [25.26]	28 [31.11]	69 [23.00]	83 [13.83]
Other	88 [88.00]	86 [78.18]	69 [76.66]	243 [81.00]	30 [26.08]	27 [28.42]	12 [13.33]	69 [23.00]	312 [52.00]
N	100	110	90	300	115	95	90	300	600

Table 19
Source of Drinking Water

	Uttar Pradesh				Uttaranchal				Total
	Azamgarh	Jhansi	Sitapur	Sub-total	Dehradun	Pithora-garh	Udham Singh Nagar	Sub-total	
Tap Water	1 [1.00]	2 [1.81]	7 [7.77]	10 [3.33]	112 [97.39]	40 [42.10]	36 [40.00]	188 [62.66]	198 [33.00]
Handpump	99 [99.00]	80 [72.72]	75 [83.33]	254 [84.66]	3 [2.72]	10 [10.52]	15 [16.66]	28 [9.33]	282 [47.00]
Dugwell	-	15 [13.63]	5 [5.55]	20 [6.66]	-	8 [8.42]	18 [20.00]	26 [8.66]	46 [7.66]
Pond/Lake/Spring	-	10 [9.09]	-	10 [3.33]	-	30 [31.57]	3 [3.33]	33 [11.00]	43 [7.16]
Others	-	3 [2.72]	1 [1.11]	4 [1.33]	-	7 [7.36]	18 [20.00]	25 [8.33]	29 [4.83]
N	100	110	90	300	115	95	90	300	600

Table 20
Type of Cooking Devices

	Uttar Pradesh				Uttaranchal				Total
	Azamgarh	Jhansi	Sitapur	Sub-total	Dehradun	Pithora-garh	Udham Singh Nagar	Sub-total	
Mud Chullha	80 [80.00]	70 [63.63]	58 [64.44]	208 [69.33]	45 [39.13]	26 [27.36]	18 [20.00]	89 [29.66]	297 [49.50]
Angeethi	3 [3.00]	15 [13.63]	2 [2.22]	20 [6.66]	-	14 [14.73]	12 [13.33]	26 [8.66]	46 [7.66]
Gas	16 [16.00]	8 [7.27]	21 [23.33]	45 [15.00]	64 [55.65]	52 [54.73]	45 [50.00]	161 [53.66]	206 [34.33]
Kerosene Stove	1 [1.00]	3 [2.72]	4 [4.44]	8 [2.66]	4 [3.47]	3 [3.15]	10 [11.11]	1 [5.66]	25 [4.16]
Electric Stove	-	-	3 [3.33]	3 [1.00]	-	-	2 [2.22]	2 [0.66]	5 [0.83]
Others	-	14 [12.72]	2 [2.22]	16 [5.33]	2 [1.73]	-	3 [3.33]	5 [1.66]	21 [3.50]
N	100	110	90	300	115	95	90	300	600

Table 21
Whether House is Electrified

	Uttar Pradesh				*Uttaranchal*				*Total*
	Azamgarh	*Jhansi*	*Sitapur*	*Sub-total*	*Dehradun*	*Pithora-garh*	*Udham Singh Nagar*	*Sub-total*	
Yes	38 [38.00]	29 [26.36]	42 [46.66]	109 [36.33]	56 [48.69]	49 [51.57]	75 [83.33]	180 [60.00]	289 [48.16]
No	62 [62.00]	81 [73.63]	48 [53.33]	191 [63.66]	59 [51.30]	46 [48.42]	15 [16.66]	120 [40.00]	311 [51.83]
N	100	110	90	300	115	95	90	300	600

are electrified. The proportion of electrified houses has been reported to be significantly high in Uttaranchal (60.0 per cent) as compared to Uttar Pradesh (36.36 per cent). 83.33 per cent respondents in Udhamsingh Nagar were enjoying electricity in their houses. The housing conditions, sanitation and living conditions were found to be more satisfactory in Uttaranchal as compared to Uttar Pradesh. These conditions have direct and indirect bearing on health status and health seeking behaviour of women and children.(Table 21).

The profile of respondents and their background simply demonstrate that most of the surveyed women belong to disadvantage classes, poor and are backward in terms of socio-economic status. The living conditions are also found to be poor however, Uttaranchal was found better placed in terms of socio-economic status as compared to Uttar Pradesh.

5

HEALTH STATUS AND HEALTH SEEKING BEHAVIOUR

In this chapter, an attempt has been made to examine the health status health practices and health seeking behaviour of women and children with the availability of health services and their access.

AVAILABILITY OF HEALTH SERVICES

The women were asked regarding awareness and availability of health services. The awareness regarding vaccination, treatment of minor diseases, and safe delivery of pregnancy, immunization, and family planning services has been reported quite satisfactory. However, only 39 per cent were found aware regarding STD/HIV/AIDS and their prevention. Only 17 per cent women were found aware regarding HIV/AIDS in Uttaranchal as against 60.33 per cent in Uttar Pradesh. Surprisingly, only 7.36 per cent women in Pithoragarh district were found aware about HIV/AIDS as against 94.54 per cent in Jhansi. It is perhaps because of the fact that social intervention on part of NGO's in the district has enhanced the knowledge level regarding the deadly disease. Overall awareness regarding health services has been reported significantly higher in Uttaranchal as compared to Uttar Pradesh (Table 1).

The main sources of information regarding availability of health services are health workers, (71.0 per cent), media (40.83

Table 1
Awareness Regarding Health Services
Source of Drinking Water

	Uttar Pradesh				*Uttaranchal*				*Total*
	Azamgarh	*Jhansi*	*Sitapur*	*Sub-total*	*Dehradun*	*Pithora-garh*	*Udham Singh Nagar*	*Sub-total*	
Treatment of miner diseases	98 [98.00]	43 [39.09]	71 [78.88]	212 [70.66]	114 [99.13]	88 [92.63]	90 [100.00]	292 [97.33]	504 [84.00]
Pre-natal care	20 [20.00]	18 [16.36]	30 [33.33]	68 [22.66]	20 [17.39]	56 [58.94]	12 [13.33]	88 [29.33]	156 [26.00]
Post-natal care	14 [14.00]	9 [8.18]	23 [25.55]	46 [15.33]	28 [24.34]	50 [52.63]	18 [20.00]	96 [32.00]	142 [23.66]
Safe delivery of Pregnancy	68 [68.00]	105 [95.45]	36 [40.00]	209 [69.66]	113 [98.26]	59 [62.10]	64 [71.11]	236 [78.66]	445 [74.16]
Vaccination	33 [33.00]	107 [97.27]	45 [50.00]	285 [95.00]	113 [98.26]	71 [74.73]	80 [88.88]	264 [88.00]	549 [91.50]
Immunization	89 [89.00]	104 [94.54]	86 [95.55]	279 [93.00]	110 [95.62]	40 [42.10]	40 [44.44]	190 [63.33]	469 [78.16]
Child care	10 [10.00]	27 [24.54]	42 [46.66]	79 [26.33]	112 [97.39]	55 [57.89]	21 [23.33]	188 [62.66]	267 [44.50]
Family Planning Services	55 [55.00]	30 [27.27]	53 [58.88]	138 [46.00]	113 [98.26]	61 [64.21]	90 [100.00]	264 [88.00]	402 [67.00]
STD/HIV/AIDS Prevention	51 [51.00]	104 [94.54]	26 [28.88]	181 [60.33]	17 [14.78]	7 [7.36]	27 [30.00]	51 [17.00]	232 [38.66]
Others	4 [4.00]	52 [47.27]	4 [4.44]	60 [20.00]	21 [18.26]	3 [3.15]	8 [8.86]	32 [10.66]	92 [15.33]
N	100	110	90	300	115	95	90	300	600

Figures given in brackets indicate percentage.

Table 2
Source of Information

	Uttar Pradesh				*Uttaranchal*				*Total*
	Azamgarh	*Jhansi*	*Sitapur*	*Sub-total*	*Dehradun*	*Pithora-garh*	*Udham Singh Nagar*	*Sub-total*	
Villagers	58 [58.00]	30 [27.27]	53 [58.88]	141 [47.00]	71 [61.73]	47 [49.47]	35 [38.88]	153 [51.00]	294 [49.00]
Relatives/Friends	25 [25.00]	19 [17.27]	29 [32.22]	73 [24.33]	73 [63.47]	40 [42.10]	48 [53.33]	161 [53.66]	234 [39.00]
Health Worker	81 [81.00]	104 [94.54]	49 [54.44]	234 [78.00]	59 [51.30]	68 [71.51]	65 [72.22]	192 [64.00]	426 [71.00]
Media	48 [48.00]	108 [98.18]	23 [25.55]	179 [59.66]	25 [21.73]	21 [22.10]	20 [22.22]	66 [22.00]	245 [40.83]
Government	12 [12.00]	106 [96.36]	10 [11.11]	128 [42.66]	15 [13.04]	23 [24.21]	42 [46.66]	80 [26.66]	208 [34.66]
Functionaries	29 [29.00]	58 [52.72]	50 [55.55]	137 [45.66]	22 [19.13]	30 [31.57]	54 [60.00]	106 [35.33]	243 [40.5]
Representative of Panchayat/ Local body									
Representative of NGOs and CBOs	22 [22.00]	2 [1.81]	35 [38.88]	59 [19.66]	1 [0.86]	24 [25.26]	64 [71.11]	89 [29.66]	148 [24.66]
Others	3 [3.00]	41 [37.27]	2 [2.22]	46 [15.33]	15 [13.04]	6 [6.31]	21 [23.33]	42 [14.00]	88 [14.66]
N	100	110	90	300	115	95	90	300	600

Figures given in brackets indicate percentage

Per cent), villages (49.0 Per cent), and relatives/ friends (39 per cent). The informal mode of information is more pronounced in Uttaranchal in comparison to Uttar Pradesh. NGO's, CBO's and Panchayats are also playing critical role in promoting the health education (Table 2).

Availability of RCH services is shown in Table 3. In the state of Uttar Pradesh, about two-fifth women reported that services for sexuality and gender information, education, and counseling (44.43 per cent), community mobilization and education for adolescent (41.66 per cent) community based contraceptive distribution (39 per cent) and motivating referral for sterilization (39.33 per cent) are available. More than one third respondents also reported that services for social marketing of contraceptives, camps for immunization, vaccination, and sterilization and referral services are available to them. Similarly, in the state of Uttaranchal most of women reported that services for sterilization, free supplies and health education is available to them, however, the proportion of respondents reporting availability of RCH devices has been comparatively low in Uttaranchal as against Uttar Pradesh (Table 3).

MARRIAGE PATTERNS

Marriage age is an important factor for analyzing the health status of women. Child marriage is still prevalent in north India and it has its bearing on health status of women. Early marriage has more chances of pregnancy and its related consequences while it enhances the mortality rates both among mothers and children. About one fourth respondents revealed that they were married off before the age of 10 years, while 37.50 per cent were married off between 11-15 years. The proportion of child marriage was found to be significantly high in Uttaranchal as against Uttar Pradesh. Thus, the proportion of respondents who were married after getting mature enough has been found to be quite low. (Table 4).

Surprisingly, most of the marriages were arranged ones which show that marriage took place with the consent of the parents which reveals prevalance of child marriage in the surveyed areas. Further majority of the respondents said that

Table 3
Availability of RCH Services

	Uttar Pradesh				*Uttaranchal*			
	Yes	*No*	*Can't say*	*N*	*Yes*	*No*	*Can't say*	*N*
Sexuality and gender information, education and counseling	134 [44.43]	161 [53.66]	5 [1.66]	300	91 [30.33]	153 [51.10]	56 [18.66]	300
Community Mobilization and education for adolescents, newly married	125 [41.66]	155 [51.66]	20 [6.66]	300	129 [43.00]	126 [42.00]	45 [15.00]	300
Community based contraceptive distribution through Panchayat, Village Council, VHG, SHGs etc.	102 [34.00]	104 [34.66]	94 [31.33]	300	55 [18.33]	211 [70.33]	34 [11.33]	300
Motivating referral for sterilization	118 [39.33]	163 [54.35]	18 [6.00]	300	69 [23.00]	178 [59.33]	53 [17.66]	300
Social marketing of condom and oral pills through Village Council, Panchayat and others	102 [34.00]	186 [62.00]	13 [4.33]	300	49 [16.33]	223 [74.33]	28 [9.33]	300
Free supplies of health services	76 [25.33]	201 [67.00]	23 [7.60]	300	125 [41.66]	156 [52.00]	19 [6.33]	300
Awareness raising for supportive care during pregnancy	76 [25.33]	201 [67.00]	23 [7.60]	300	122 [40.66]	130 [43.33]	48 [16.00]	300
Mobilizing community support for transport, referral and blood donation	67 [22.33]	205 [68.33]	28 [9.33]	300	67 [22.33]	163 [54.33]	70 [23.33]	300
Early detection and referral of high risk pregnancy	74 [24.66]	195 [65.00]	31 [10.33]	300	77 [25.66]	154 [51.33]	69 [23.00]	300
Delivery Planning	91 [30.33]	183 [61.00]	26 [8.66]	300	79 [26.33]	127 [42.33]	94 [31.33]	300

	Uttar Pradesh				*Uttaranchal*			
	Yes	*No*	*Can't say*	*N*	*Yes*	*No*	*Can't say*	*N*
Referral for detecting complications to hospital	97 [32.33]	174 [58.00]	29 [9.66]	300	68 [22.66]	130 [43.33]	102 [34.00]	300
Providing transport referral	93 [31.00]	183 [61.00]	24 [8.00]	300	46 [15.33]	155 [51.66]	99 [33.00]	300
Camps for immunization and vaccination	110 [36.66]	162 [54.00]	28 [9.33]	300	174 [58.00]	78 [26.00]	48 [16.00]	300
Camps for sterilization	97 [32.33]	161 [53.66]	42 [14.00]	300	137 [45.66]	97 [32.33]	66 [22.00]	300
Camps for promoting Couple Protection Rate	82 [27.33]	193 [64.33]	25 [8.33]	300	50 [16.66]	116 [38.66]	134 [44.66]	300
Others	78 [26.00]	176 [58.66]	46 [15.33]	300	65 [21.66]	92 [30.66]	143 [47.66]	300

Figures given in brackets indicate percentage

Table 4
Marriage Patterns

		Uttar Pradesh			Uttaranchal			Total
		Male	*Female*	*Sub-total*	*Male*	*Female*	*Sub-total*	
Age of marriage	Less then 10 years		19 [6.33]			21 [7.00]		40 [6.67]
	11 -15 years		19 [6.33]			24 [8.00]		43 [7.17]
	15 -18 years		48 [16.00]			46 [15.33]		94 [15.67]
	18 -21 years		165 [55.00]			160 [53.33]		325 [54.17]
	More then 21 years		49 [16.33]			49 [16.33]		98 [16.33]
	N		300			300		600
Type of marriage	Arranged		295 [98.33]			279 [93.00]		574 [95.67]
	Contract		-			-		-
	Love		2 [6.67]			5 [1.67]		7 [1.17]
	Others		3 [1.00]			16 [5.33]		19 [3.17]
	N		300			300		600
Nature of marriage	Inter-caste		5 [1.67]			13 [4.33]		18 [3.00]
	Inter-religion		1 [0.33]			2 [0.67]		3 [0.50]
	Within caste/group		291 [97.00]			280 [93.33]		571 [95.17]
	Others		3[1.00]			5[1.67]		8[1.33]
	N		300			300		600

Figures given in brackets indicate percentage.

they were married off within their communities. Only 3.50 per cent marriages were inter caste or inter-religion.

Age wise type of marriage is shown in Table 5. The arranged marriages have taken place at early age while other types were performed after getting maturity of age. Arranged marriages were mainly within groups or castes while inter-caste and inter-religion marriages took place in the age of maturity (Table 6).

Thus it is clear that inter-caste and inter-relation marriages took place after getting maturity of age. Type of marriage and nature of marriage relationship is shown in Table 7.

Most of the arranged marriages were within community while love marriages were out side the community. District wise age at marriage is given in Table 8.

The child marriage was found to be more pronouncing in Uttaranchal as compared to Uttar Pradesh. The proportion of child marriage is reported to be higher in Jhansi, Pithoragarh and Udhamsingh Nagar. About 60.50 per cent respondents accepted that they were married after attaining the age of 18 years and above.

The respondents were asked regarding consultation of health issues. The counselors, family members, relatives and friends were reported the main persons whom respondents committed for health matters. However, the role of counselors and doctors has been reported to be limited. Moreover, consultation for reproductive and sexual health with doctors has been reported to be very nominal. Further people are very hesitant to discuss health issues within their family (Table 9).

In the state of Uttaranchal, respondents consult counselors and doctors for general and reproductive and sexual health. Respondents also reported that they discuss health issues among their families (Table 10).

HEALTH CARE DURING PREGNANCY

The respondents were asked regarding visit of health workers for antenatal checkup. About two fifth respondents reported that health workers visited their homes for antenatal checkup. It was found more pronouncing in Sitapur (50 per cent) and

Table 5
Age wise Type of Marriage

	Uttar Pradesh					Uttaranchal					Total
	Arranged	*Contract*	*Love*	*Others*	*Sub-total*	*Arranged*	*Contract*	*Love*	*Others*	*Sub-total*	
Less then 10 years	19 [6.44]	-	-	-	19 [6.33]	21 [7.00]	-	-	-	21 [7.00]	40 [6.67]
11 -15 years	19 [6.44]	-	-	-	19 [6.33]	21 [7.00]	-	-	3 [18.75]	24 [8.00]	43 [7.17]
15 -18 years	48 [16.27]	-	-	-	48 [16.00]	43 [15.41]	-	-	3 [18.75]	46 [15.33]	94 [15.67]
18 -21 years	162 [54.92]	-	2 [100.00]	1 [33.33]	165 [55.00]	149 [53.41]	-	5 [100.00]	6 [37.50]	160 [53.33]	325 [54.17]
More then 21 years	47 [15.93]	-	-	2 [66.67]	49 [16.33]	45 [16.13]	-	-	4 [25.00]	49 [16.33]	98 [16.33]
N	295		2	3	30	279	-	5	16	30	600

Figures given in brackets indicate percentage

Table 6
Age wise Nature of Marriage

	Uttar Pradesh					Uttaranchal					Total
	Inter-caste	*Inter-religion*	*Within caste/group*	*Others*	*Sub-total*	*Inter-caste*	*Inter-religion*	*Within caste/group*	*Others*	*Sub-total*	
Less then 10 years	-	-	19 [6.53]	-	19 [6.33]	-	-	21 [7.50]	-	21 [7.00]	24 [6.67]
11 -15 years	-	-	19 [6.53]	-	19 [6.33]	-	-	24 [8.57]	-	24 [8.00]	43 [7.17]
15 -18 years	-	-	48 [16.49]	-	48 [16.00]	3 [23.08]	-	43 [15.36]	-	46 [15.33]	94 [15.67]
18 -21 years	4 [80.00]	-	159 [54.64]	2 [66.67]	165 [55.00]	6 [46.15]	-	151 [53.93]	3 [60.00]	160 [53.33]	325 [54.17]
More then 21 years	1 [20.00]	1 [100.00]	46 [15.81]	1 [33.33]	49 [16.33]	4 [30.77]	2 [100.00]	41 [14.64]	2 [40.00]	49 [16.33]	98 [16.00]
N	5	1	291	3	300	13	2	280	5	300	600

Figures given in brackets indicate percentage

Table 7
Type of Marriage with Nature of Marriage

	Uttar Pradesh					Uttaranchal					Total
	Arranged	*Contract*	*Love*	*Others*	*Sub-total*	*Arranged*	*Contract*	*Love*	*Others*	*Sub-total*	
Inter-caste	5 [1.69]	-	-	-	5 [1.67]	8 [2.87]	-	2 [40.00]	3 [18.75]	13 [43.33]	18 [3.00]
Inter-religion	-	-	1 [50.00]	-	1 [0.33]	1 [0.36]	-	-	1 [6.25]	2 [0.67]	3 [0.50]
Within caste/ group	288 [97.63]	-	1 [50.00]	2 [66.67]	291 [97.00]	270 [96.68]	-	1 [20.00]	9 [56.25]	280 [93.33]	571 [95.17]
Others	2 [0.68]	-	-	1 [33.33]	3 [1.00]	-	-	2 [40.00]	3 [18.75]	5 [1.67]	8 [1.33]
N	295	0	2	3	300	279	0	5	16	300	600

Figures given in brackets indicate percentage

Table 8
Age at Marriage of Respondent

	Uttar Pradesh				Uttaranchal				Total
	Azamgarh	*Jhansi*	*Sitapur*	*sub-total*	*Dehradun*	*Pithoragarh*	*Udham Singh Nagar*	*Sub-total*	
Less then 10 years	6 [9.09]	9 [7.76]	4 [4.71]	19 [6.33]	6 [6.19]	10 [8.47]	5 [5.88]	21 [7.00]	40 [6.67]
11 -15 years	5 [5.05]	11 [9.48]	3 [3.53]	19 [6.33]	5 [5.15]	13 [11.02]	6 [7.06]	24 [8.00]	43 [7.17]
15 -18 years	15 [15.15]	20 [17.24]	13 [15.29]	48 [16.00]	13 [13.40]	18 [15.25]	15 [17.65]	46 [15.33]	94 [15.67]
18 -21 years	56 [56.57]	59 [50.86]	50 [58.82]	165 [55.00]	59 [60.82]	56 [47.46]	45 [52.94]	160 [53.33]	325 [54.17]
More then 21 years	17 [17.17]	17 [14.66]	15 [17.65]	49 [16.33]	14 [14.43]	21 [17.80]	14 [16.47]	49 [16.33]	98 [16.33]
N	99	116	85	300	97	118	85	300	600

Figures given in brackets indicate percentage.

Table 9

Consultation of Health Issues with Counselors in Uttar Pradesh

	Family Members	*Relatives*	*Friends*	*Counselors*		*Doctors*	*N*
				Individual	*Institutional*		
General Health	300 [100.00]	210 [70.00]	160 [53.33]	60 [20.00]	76 [25.33]	80 [26.67]	300
Nutrition	296 [98.67]	215 [71.66]	85 [71.67]	76 [25.33]	96 [32.00]	90 [30.00]	300
Reproductive Health	200 [66.67]	175 [58.33]	125 [41.67]	95 [31.67]	125 [41.67]	110 [36.67]	300
Sexual Health	125 [41.67]	150 [50.00]	85 [28.33]	30 [10.00]	25 [8.33]	15 [5.00]	300
Friendship	300 [100.00]	275 [91.67]	300 [100.00]	15 [5.00]	24 [8.00]	28 [9.33]	300
Marriage	275 [91.67]	215 [71.67]	300 [100.00]	24 [8.00]	-	15 [5.00]	300
Education	300 [100.00]	300 [100.00]	300 [100.00]	10 [3.33]	25 [8.33]	-	300
Others	125 [41.67]	164 [54.67]	120 [40.00]	-	-	25 [8.33]	300
Total	1921 [80.24]	1704 [71.00]	1475 [61.46]	310 [12.92]	371 [15.46]	363 [15.13]	2400

Figures given in brackets indicate percentage.

Table 10
Consultation of Health Issues with Counselors in Uttaranchal

	Family Members	*Relatives*	*Friends*	*Counselors*		*Doctors*	*N*
				Individual	*Institutional*		
General Health	300 [100.00]	225 [75.00]	240 [80.00]	165 [55.00]	275 [91.67]	300 [100.00]	300
Nutrition	225 [75.00]	235 [78.33]	280 [93.33]	126 [42.00]	180 [60.00]	300 [100.00]	300
Reproductive Health	25 [8.33]	15 [5.00]	290 [96.67]	100 [33.33]	35 [11.67]	198 [66.00]	300
Sexual Health	65 [21.67]	125 [41.67]	295 [98.33]	75 [25.00]	45 [15.00]	215 [71.67]	300
Friendship	300 [100.00]	245 [81.67]	300 [100.00]	-	-	-	300
Marriage	125 [41.67]	175 [58.33]	300 [100.00]	-	-	-	300
Education	300 [100.00]	230 [76.67]	300 [100.00]	45 [15.00]	65 [21.67]	-	300
Others	175 [58.33]	125 [41.67]	115 [38.33]	48 [16.00]	52 [17.33]	70 [23.33]	300
N	1515 [63.13]	1375 [57.29]	2120 [88.33]	559 [23.29]	652 [27.17]	1083 [45.13]	2400

Figures given in brackets indicate percentage.

Table 11
Visit of Health Workers for Antenatal Checkup

	Uttar Pradesh				*Uttaranchal*				*Total*
	Azamgarh	*Jhansi*	*Sitapur*	*Sub-total*	*Dehradun*	*Pithora-garh*	*Udham Singh Nagar*	*Sub-total*	
Yes	33 [33.00]	46 [41.82]	45 [50.00]	124 [41.33]	36 [31.30]	47 [49.47]	39 [43.33]	122 [40.67]	246 [41.00]
No	67 [67.00]	64 [58.18]	45 [50.00]	176 [58.67]	79 [68.70]	48 [50.53]	51 [56.67]	178 [59.33]	354 [59.00]
N	100	110	90	300	115	95	90	300	600
If yes how many time visit									
One	8 [24.24]	18 [39.13]	20 [44.44]	46 [37.10]	12 [33.33]	23 [48.94]	15 [38.46]	50 [40.98]	96 [39.02]
Two	10 [30.30]	14 [30.43]	13 [28.89]	37 [29.84]	11 [30.56]	10 [21.28]	9 [23.08]	30 [24.59]	67 [27.24]
Three	5 [15.15]	10 [21.74]	7 [15.56]	22 [17.74]	9 [25.00]	6 [12.77]	10 [25.64]	25 [20.49]	47 [19.11]
Four	6 [18.18]	4 [8.70]	5 [11.11]	15 [12.09]	4 [11.11]	5 [10.64]	3 [7.69]	12 [9.84]	27 [10.98]
More than Five	4 [12.12]	-	-	4 [3.23]	-	3 [6.38]	2 [5.13]	5 [4.10]	9 [3.66]
N	33	46	45	124	36	47	39	122	246

Figures given in brackets indicate percentage.

Pithoragarh (49.47 per cent) while it was recorded as low as 33 per cent in Azamgarh district. In most of the cases visit by health workers has been reported one or two times (Table 11).

About three fourth respondents admitted that they went for health checkup. The proportion of such women respondents has been found higher in Uttar Pradesh (81.67 per cent) as compared to Uttaranchal (67.0 per cent). It is because of the fact that facilities for health checkup in the state of Uttar Pradesh are comparatively better and people have good access to such facilities while in the state of Uttaranchal, difficult and tough terrain create hurdles in easy access to government run health facilities and services. Those who did not avail the antenatal checkup said that services were not available at time (66.23 per cent), poor quality of services (61.69 per cent) and not necessary (55.19 per cent) for them. Importantly, a large proportion of respondents reported that antenatal checkup was not customary to their families (46.1 per cent). It was found more pronouncing in Azamgarh (71.43 per cent) followed by Sitapur (70.0 per cent) and Dehradun (55.56 per cent). Poor quality of services was reported high in Dehradun and Pithoragarh district (Table 12).

Occupation wise antenatal check up is shown in Table 13. Antenatal check up is found more among the respondents whose main occupation is agriculture and agricultural labour. However, in the state of Uttaranchal, mainly service class women availed this facility (48.30 per cent). The business class women also availed this facility to the substantial extent (24.87 per cent).

Caste wise antenatal checkup is shown in Table 14. In the state of Uttar Pradesh, it was reported to be higher among OBC's (57.96 per cent) while in the state of Uttaranchal it was reported higher among general castes (44.28 per cent).

Income wise antenatal checkup is given in Table 15. In the state of Uttar Pradesh, it has been recorded higher among women belonging to high income group while in the state of Uttaranchal, it is found to be higher in low income group respondents.

Table 12
Antenatal Checkup

	Uttar Pradesh				*Uttaranchal*				*Total*
	Azamgarh	*Jhansi*	*Sitapur*	*Sub-total*	*Dehradun*	*Pithora-garh*	*Udham Singh Nagar*	*Sub-total*	
Yes	79 [79.00]	96 [87.27]	70 [77.78]	245 [81.67]	88 [76.52]	68 [71.58]	45 [50.00]	201 [67.00]	446 [74.33]
No	21 [21.00]	14 [12.73]	20 [22.22]	55 [18.33]	27 [23.48]	27 [28.42]	45 [50.00]	99 [33.00]	154 [25.67]
N	100	110	90	300	115	95	90	300	600
If no, what is the reason									
Lack of knowledge of services	20 [95.24]	10 [71.43]	12 [60.00]	42 [76.26]	8 [29.63]	7 [25.93]	20 [44.44]	35 [35.35]	77 [50.00]
Not necessary	19 [90.47]	5 [35.71]	13 [65.00]	37 [67.27]	24 [88.89]	12 [44.44]	12 [26.67]	48 [48.48]	85 [55.19]
Not Customary	15 [71.43]	4 [28.57]	14 [70.00]	33 [60.00]	15 [55.56]	16 [59.26]	7 [15.56]	38 [38.38]	71 [46.10]
Financial cost	10 [47.62]	6 [42.86]	16 [80.00]	32 [58.18]	18 [66.67]	10 [37.04]	8 [17.78]	36 [36.36]	68 [44.16]
Inconvenient	12 [57.14]	10 [71.43]	4 [20.00]	26 [47.27]	20 [74.07]	20 [74.07]	10 [22.22]	50 [50.51]	76 [49.35]
Poor quality of services	13 [61.90]	9 [64.29]	18 [90.00]	40 [72.73]	21 [77.78]	25 [92.59]	9 [20.00]	55 [55.56]	95 [61.69]
No time	18 [85.71]	3 [21.43]	16 [80.00]	37 [67.27]	25 [92.59]	20 [74.07]	20 [44.44]	65 [65.66]	102 [66.23]
Not permitted to go outside	5 [23.81]	2 [14.29]	2 [10.00]	9 [16.36]	4 [14.81]	15 [55.56]	12 [26.67]	31 [31.31]	40 [25.97]
Others	21 [100.00]	5 [35.71]	13 [65.00]	39 [70.91]	9 [33.33]	7 [25.93]	7 [15.56]	23 [23.23]	62 [40.26]
N	21	14	20	55	27	27	45	99	154

Figures given in brackets indicate percentage.

Table 13
Occupation wise Antenatal Checkup

	Uttar Pradesh Antenatal checkup			*Uttaranchal Antenatal checkup*		
	Yes	*No*	*Sub-total*	*Yes*	*No*	*Sub-total*
Agriculture	157 [64.08]	23 [41.82]	180 [60.00]	28 [13.93]	52 [52.52]	80 [26.67]
Business	7 [2.86]	1 [1.82]	8 [2.67]	50 [24.87]	9 [9.09]	59 [19.67]
Service	12 [4.90]	-	12 [4.00]	81 [40.30]	5 [5.05]	86 [28.67]
Labour	65 [26.53]	31 [56.36]	96 [32.00]	6 [2.99]	28 [28.28]	34 [11.33]
Others	4 [1.63]	-	4 [1.33]	36 [17.91]	5 [5.05]	41 [13.67]
N	245	55	300	201	99	300

Figures given in brackets indicate percentage.

Table 14
Caste wise Antenatal Checkup

	Uttar Pradesh Antenatal checkup			*Uttaranchal Antenatal checkup*		
	Yes	*No*	*Sub-total*	*Yes*	*No*	*Sub-total*
General	45 [18.37]	3 [5.45]	48 [16.00]	89 [44.28]	53 [53.54]	142 [47.33]
OBC	142 [57.96]	21 [38.18]	163 [54.33]	68 [33.83]	18 [18.18]	86 [28.67]
SC	48 [19.59]	20 [36.36]	68 [22.67]	13 [6.47]	12 [12.12]	25 [8.33]
ST	-	2 [3.63]	2 [0.67]	1 [0.50]	4 [4.04]	5 [1.67]
Muslim	10 [4.08]	9 [16.36]	19 [6.33]	5 [2.49]	2 [2.02]	7 [2.33]
Others	-	-	-	25 [12.44]	10 [10.10]	35 [11.67]
N	245	55	300	201	99	300

Figures given in brackets indicate percentage.

Table 15
Income level wise Antenatal Checkup

	Uttar Pradesh Antenatal checkup			*Uttaranchal Antenatal checkup*		
	Yes	*No*	*Sub-total*	*Yes*	*No*	*Sub-total*
Less then 25000	56 [22.86]	23 [41.82]	79 [26.33]	7 [3.48]	33 [33.33]	43 [14.33]
25000-50000	63 [25.71]	13 [23.64]	76 [25.33]	58 [28.86]	18 [18.18]	76 [25.33]
50000-75000	65 [26.53]	7 [12.73]	72 [24.00]	40 [19.90]	26 [26.26]	63 [21.00]
75000-100000	51 [20.82]	10 [18.18]	61 [20.33]	56 [27.86]	13 [13.13]	69 [23.00]
More then 100000	10 [4.08]	2 [3.64]	12 [4.00]	40 [19.90]	9 [9.09]	49 [16.33]
N	245	55	300	201	99	300

Figures given in brackets indicate percentage.

The respondents were asked whether they were given folic acid tablets during their pregnancy. About three fourth respondents admitted that they were given folic tablets. It was found more pronouncing in Uttar Pradesh as compared to Uttaranchal. Again, this proportion was recorded comparatively higher in Azamgarh (64.00 per cent) and Jhansi (60.00 per cent) while it was reported as low as 49.47 per cent in Pithoragarh (Table 16).

The respondents were asked whether they received injection to prevent them and their baby from convulsion. About two third respondents reported that they received such injection. It was found more pronouncing in Dehradun (88.70 per cent) and Azamgarh district (80 per cent) whereas it was reported as low as 36.67 per cent in Sitapur (Table 17).

The place of delivery is shown in Table 18. More than half of women reported that they delivered their pregnancy at home. It was reported high in Azamgarh (60.00 per cent) and Udhamsingh Nagar (53.33 per cent). However, institutional deliveries were reported to be quite high i.e. less than 60 per cent. Again, the proportion on non-government run health centres was found to be quite significant in Azamgarh and Sitapur.

Education wise delivery of pregnancy is shown in Table 19. Those who are educated prefer to deliver their pregnancy at safe place i.e. institutions of repute. It is also true in case of the present study that well educated women delivered their pregnancy at district hospitals and nursing homes. In the state of Uttaranchal, highly educated women also delivered their pregnancy at PHC's/CHC's and district hospitals or private hospitals (Table 20).

Age wise place of delivery in Uttar Pradesh is given in Table 21. The aged respondents delivered their pregnancy at home while growing age respondents admitted that they delivered their pregnancy at hospitals. It is because of the fact that chances of delivery complications are higher among young persons and particularly during first pregnancy while the chances of complications in second or third delivery are lower and therefore older women may take risk to deliver their pregnancy at home (Table 22).

Table 16
Whether You Were Given Iron Folic Tablets

	Uttar Pradesh				*Uttaranchal*				*Total*
	Azamgarh	*Jhansi*	*Sitapur*	*Sub-total*	*Dehradun*	*Pithora-garh*	*Udham Singh Nagar*	*Sub-total*	
Yes	64 [64.00]	66 [60.00]	51 [56.67]	181 [60.33]	65 [56.52]	47 [49.47]	56 [62.22]	168 [56.00]	349 [58.17]
No	36 [36.00]	44 [40.00]	39 [43.33]	119 [39.67]	50 [43.48]	48 [50.53]	34 [37.78]	132 [44.00]	251 [41.83]
N	100	110	90	300	115	95	90	300	600

Figures given in brackets indicate percentage.

Table 17
Receiving of Injections to Prevent Baby from Convulsion

	Uttar Pradesh				*Uttaranchal*				*Total*
	Azamgarh	*Jhansi*	*Sitapur*	*Sub-total*	*Dehradun*	*Pithora-garh*	*Udham Singh Nagar*	*Sub-total*	
Yes	80 [80.00]	74 [67.27]	33 [36.67]	187 [62.33]	102 [88.70]	59 [62.11]	50 [55.56]	211 [70.33]	398 [66.33]
No	20 [20.00]	36 [32.73]	57 [63.33]	113 [37.67]	13 [11.30]	36 [37.89]	40 [44.44]	89 [29.67]	202 [33.67]
N	100	110	90	300	115	95	90	300	600

Figures given in brackets indicate percentage

Table 18
Where did you give birth

	Uttar Pradesh				*Uttaranchal*				*Total*
	Azamgarh	*Jhansi*	*Sitapur*	*Sub-total*	*Dehradun*	*Pithora-garh*	*Udham Singh Nagar*	*Sub-total*	
Home	60 [60.00]	64 [58.18]	47 [52.22]	171 [57.00]	59 [51.30]	46 [48.42]	48 [53.33]	153 [51.00]	324 [54.00]
Municipal Hospital	3 [3.00]	-	-	3 [1.00]	7 [6.09]	2 [2.11]	3 [3.33]	12 [4.00]	15 [2.50]
PHC/CHC	12 [12.00]	15 [13.64]	12 [13.33]	39 [13.00]	10 [8.70]	9 [9.47]	10 [11.11]	29 [9.67]	68 [11.33]
Sub-centre	-	-	-	-	-	1 [1.05]	-	1 [0.33]	1 [0.17]
District Hospital	-	14 [12.73]	18 [20.00]	32 [10.67]	21 [18.26]	18 [18.95]	16 [17.78]	55 [18.33]	87 [14.50]
Private Hospital or Nursing Home	25 [25.00]	17 [15.45]	13 [14.44]	55 [18.33]	18 [15.65]	19 [20.00]	13 [14.44]	50 [16.67]	105 [17.50]
Others	-	-	-	-	-	-	-	-	-
N	100	110	90	300	115	95	90	300	600

Figures given in brackets indicate percentage.

Table 19
Education wise Place of Delivery in Uttar Pradesh

	Uttar Pradesh								*Total*
	Illiterate	*Literate*	*Upto Primary*	*Jr. High School*	*Inter-mediate*	*Graduate*	*Post Graduate*	*Other*	
Home	36 [66.67]	36 [75.00]	22 [55.00]	32 [57.14]	27 [52.94]	12 [40.00]	2 [13.33]	4 [66.67]	171 [57.00]
Municipal Hospital	-	-	-	-	1 [1..96]	2 [6.67]	-	-	3 [1.00]
PHC/CHC	5 [9.26]	5 [10.42]	7 [17.50]	8 [14.29]	10 [19.61]	2 [6.67]	2 [13.33]	-	39 [13.00]
Sub-centre	-	-	-	-	-	-	-	-	-
District Hospital	2 [3.70]	3 [6.25]	5 [12.50]	7 [12.50]	5 [9.80]	4 [13.33]	6 [40.00]	-	32 [10.67]
Private Hospital or Nursing Home	11 [20.37]	4 [8.33]	6 [15.00]	9 [16.07]	8 [15.69]	10 [33.33]	5 [33.33]	2 [33.33]	55 [18.33]
Others	-	-	-	-	-	-	-	-	-
N	54	48	40	56	51	30	15	6	300

Figures given in brackets indicate percentage.

Table 20
Education wise Place of Delivery in Uttaranchal

	Uttar Pradesh								*Total*
	Illiterate	*Literate*	*Upto Primary*	*Jr. High School*	*Inter-mediate*	*Graduate*	*Post Graduate*	*Other*	
Home	23 [54.76]	23 [57.5]	20 [51.28]	34 [68.00]	26 [47.27]	16 [38.09]	9 [36.00]	2 [28.57]	153 [51.00]
Municipal Hospital	1 [2.38]	-	4 [10.25]	2 [4.00]	3 [5.45]	2 [4..76]	-	-	12 [4.00]
PHC/CHC	8 [19.04]	4 [10.00]	4 [10.25]	3 [6.00]	5 [9.09]	2 [4..76]	3 [12.00]	-	29 [9.66]
Sub-centre	-	-	-	-	1 [1.81]	-	-	-	1 [0.33]
District Hospital	6 [14.28]	6 [15.00]	5 [12.82]	3 [6.00]	9 [16.36]	15 [35.71]	8 [32.00]	3 [42.85]	55 [18.33]
Private Hospital or Nursing Home	4 [9.52]	7 [17.50]	6 [15.38]	8 [16.00]	11 [20.00]	7 [16.66]	5 [20.00]	2 [28.57]	50 [16.66]
Others	-	-	-	.	-	-	-	-	-
N	42	40	39	50	55	43	25	7	300

Figures given in brackets indicate percentage.

Table 21
Age-wise Place of Delivery in Uttar Pradesh

	Uttar Pradesh						*Total*
	Less than 18 Year	*19-25 year*	*26-35 year*	*36-45 year*	*46-55 year*	*55 to above*	
Home	1 [10.00]	33 [45.83]	43 [55.84]	46 [63.01]	5 [20.00]	43 [100.00]	171 [57.00]
Municipal Hospital	-	-	3 [3.89]	-	-	-	3 [1.00]
PHC/CHC	2 [20.00]	20 [27.77]	5 [6.49]	5 [6..84]	7 [28.00]	-	39 [13.00]
Sub-centre	-	-	-	-	-	-	-
District Hospital	3 [30.00]	3 [4.16]	8 [10.38]	12 [16.43]	6 [24.00]	-	32 [10.66]
Private Hospital or Nursing Home	4 [40.00]	16 [22.22]	18 [23.37]	10 [13.69]	7 [28.00]	-	55 [18.33]
Others	-	-	-	-	-	-	-
N	10	72	77	73	25	43	300

Figures given in brackets indicate percentage

Table 22
Age-wise Place of Delivery in Uttaranchal

	Uttaranchal						*Total*
	Less than 18 Year	*19-25 year*	*26-35 year*	*36-45 year*	*46-55 year*	*55 to above*	
Home	9 [37.50]	27 [48.21]	34 [44.15]	10 [62.50]	22 [40.74]	21 [84.00]	153 [51.00]
Municipal Hospital	-	1 [1.78]	6 [7.79]	2 [3.12]	3 [5.55]	-	12 [4.00]
PHC/CHC	2 [8.33]	6 [10.71]	8 [10.38]	3 [4.68]	9 [16.66]	1 [4.00]	29 [9.66]
Sub-centre	-	1 [1.78]	-	-	-	-	1 [0.33]
District Hospital	5 [20.83]	11 [19.64]	18 [23.37]	12 [18.75]	8 [14.81]	1 [4.00]	55 [18.33]
Private Hospital or Nursing Home	8 [33.33]	10 [17.85]	11 [14.28]	7 [10.93]	12 [22.22]	2 [8.00]	50 [16.66]
Others	-	-	-	-	-	-	-
N	24	56	77	64	54	25	300

Figures given in brackets indicate percentage.

Table 23
Assistance in Delivery

	Uttar Pradesh				*Uttaranchal*				*Total*
	Azamgarh	*Jhansi*	*Sitapur*	*Sub-total*	*Dehradun*	*Pithora-garh*	*Udham Singh Nagar*	*Sub-total*	
Doctor	8 [8.00]	12 [10.90]	10 [11.11]	30 [10.00]	13 [11.30]	9 [9.47]	16 [17.77]	38 [12.66]	68 [11.33]
Nurse	19 [19.00]	26 [23.63]	19 [21.11]	64 [21.33]	15 [13.63]	11 [11.57]	13 [14.44]	39 [13.00]	103 [17.16]
ANM/LHV	15 [15.00]	10 [9.09]	11 [12.22]	36 [12.00]	9 [7.82]	12 [12.63]	9 [10.00]	30 [10.00]	66 [11.00]
Trained Traditional Birth Attendant	15 [15.00]	13 [11.81]	12 [13.33]	40 [13.33]	19 [16.52]	21 [22.10]	15 [16.66]	55 [18.33]	95 [15.83]
Untrained Dai	30 [30.00]	28 [25.45]	28 [31.11]	86 [28.66]	46 [40.00]	20 [21.05]	29 [32.22]	95 [31.66]	181 [30.16]
Relatives/Friends	11 [11.00]	15 [13.63]	10 [11.11]	36 [12.00]	9 [7.82]	13 [13.68]	6 [6.66]	28 [9.33]	64 [10.66]
Others	2 [2.00]	6 [5.45]	-	8 [2.66]	4 [3.47]	9 [9.47]	2 [2.22]	15 [5.00]	23 [3.83]
N	100	110	90	300	115	95	90	300	600

Figures given in brackets indicate percentage.

The respondents were asked about the assistance received during their deliveries. In most of the cases qualified doctors, nurses and mid wives assisted in safe delivery however, about 12 per cent respondents admitted that they were assisted by their relatives and friends as well as untrained dais (Table 23).

About two fifth respondents revealed that they faced complications during their delivery of pregnancy. It was found more pronouncing in Jhansi (58.18 per cent) followed by Sitapur (53.33 per cent), However, this proportion was reported least in Dehradun. The women further revealed that they faced problems of excessive bleeding (28.22 per cent) and long period of labour (19.92 per cent). The cases of excessive bleeding were reported to be high in Udhamsingh Nagar (Table 24).

The respondents were further asked regarding delivery complications induced diseases. Most of them said that they faced problems of delivery complications however; no major disease was reported except in a few cases of distortion of tract (Table 25).

Most of the respondents accepted that they breast fed their babies (84.0 per cent). It was reported higher in Jhansi (92.77 per cent) and Azamgarh (92.0 per cent) while only 69.47 per cent women breastfed to their children in Pithoragarh (Table 26).

FERTILITY-PREFERENCES

The respondents were asked whether their husbands approve use of family planning method. Less than 60 per cent respondents reported that their husbands approve adoption of family planning measures. This was found more pronouncing in Azamgarh (68.00 per cent) followed by Dehradun (68.69 per cent) while it was found least in Udhamsingh Nagar (44.44 per cent). About 18 per cent respondents were not in position to comment on this question (Table 27).

The respondents were further asked about the frequency of discussion about family planning. About two third respondents said that their husbands talk once or twice regarding family planning methods. About 41.33 per cent

Table 24
Complication in Delivery
Assistance in Delivery

	Uttar Pradesh				*Uttaranchal*				*Total*
	Azamgarh	*Jhansi*	*Sitapur*	*Sub-total*	*Dehradun*	*Pithora-garh*	*Udham Singh Nagar*	*Sub-total*	
Yes	42 [42.00]	64 [58.18]	48 [53.33]	154 [51.33]	23 [20.00]	30 [31.58]	34 [37.78]	87 [29.00]	241 [40.17]
No	58 [58.00]	46 [41.82]	42 [46.67]	146 [48.67]	92 [80.00]	65 [68.42]	56 [62.22]	213 [71.00]	354 [59.83]
N	100	110	90	300	115	95	90	300	600
If Yes									
Excessive bleeding	17 [40.48]	2 [3.13]	21 [43.75]	40 [25.97]	3 [13.04]	10 [33.33]	15 [44.12]	28 [32.18]	68 [28.22]
Long period of labour	5 [11.90]	-	8 [16.67]	13 [8.44]	12 [52.17]	12 [40.00]	11 [32.35]	35 [40.23]	48 [19.92]
Delayed delivery of Placenta	4 [9.52]	8 [12.50]	4 [8.33]	16 [10.39]	1 [4.25]	-	2 [5.88]	3 [3.45]	19 [7.88]
Others	16 [38.10]	54 [84.38]	15 [10.42]	70 [45.45]	7 [30.43]	8 [26.67]	6 [17.65]	21 [24.14]	91 [37.76]
N	42	64	48	154	23	30	34	87	241

Figures given in brackets indicate percentage.

Table 25
Whether Delivery Complication Recorded in Diseases

	Uttar Pradesh				*Uttaranchal*				*Total*
	Azamgarh	*Jhansi*	*Sitapur*	*Sub-total*	*Dehradun*	*Pithora-garh*	*Udham Singh Nagar*	*Sub-total*	
Distortion of tract	15 [35.71]	5 [7.81]	3 [6.25]	23 [14.94]	2 [8.70]	3 [10.00]	6 [17.65]	11 [12.66]	34 [14.11]
Disfiguring of ovary/uterus	3 [7.14]	2 [3.13]	8 [16.67]	13 [8.44]	4 [17.29]	5 [16.67]	3 [8.82]	12 [13.79]	25 [10.37]
Others	24 [57.14]	57 [89.06]	37 [77.08]	118 [76.62]	17 [73.91]	22 [73.33]	25 [73.53]	64 [73.56]	182 [75.52]
N	42	64	48	154	23	30	34	87	241

Figures given in brackets indicate percentage.

Table 26
Did You Ever Breast Feed

	Uttar Pradesh				*Uttaranchal*				*Total*
	Azamgarh	*Jhansi*	*Sitapur*	*Sub-total*	*Dehradun*	*Pithora-garh*	*Udham Singh Nagar*	*Sub-total*	
Yes	92 [92.00]	107 [97.27]	80 [88.89]	279 [93.00]	90 [78.26]	66 [69.47]	69 [76.67]	225 [75.00]	504 [84.00]
No	8 [8.00]	3 [2.73]	10 [11.11]	21 [7.00]	25 [21.74]	29 [30.53]	21 [23.33]	75 [25.00]	96 [16.00]
N	100	110	90	300	115	95	90	300	600

Figures given in brackets indicate percentage.

Table 27
Family Planning Method

	Uttar Pradesh				*Uttaranchal*				*Total*
	Azamgarh	*Jhansi*	*Sitapur*	*Sub-total*	*Dehradun*	*Pithora-garh*	*Udham Singh Nagar*	*Sub-total*	
Approves	68 [68.00]	70 [63.64]	49 [54.44]	187 [62.33]	79 [68.69]	46 [48.42]	40 [44.44]	165 [55.00]	352 [58.67]
Disapproves	17 [17.00]	21 [19.09]	24 [26.67]	62 [20.67]	30 [26.08]	29 [38.52]	21 [23.33]	80 [26.66]	142 [23.67]
Do not Know	15 [15.00]	19 [17.27]	17 [18.89]	51 [17.00]	6 [5.21]	20 [21.05]	29 [32.22]	55 [18.33]	106 [17.67]
N	100	110	90	300	115	95	90	300	600

Figures given in brackets indicate percentage.

Table 28
How often you Talked to Your Husband About Family Planning

	Uttar Pradesh				*Uttaranchal*				*Total*
	Azamgarh	*Jhansi*	*Sitapur*	*Sub-total*	*Dehradun*	*Pithora-garh*	*Udham Singh Nagar*	*Sub-total*	
Never	32 [32.00]	40 [36.36]	41 [45.56]	113 [37.67]	36 [31.30]	49 [51.58]	50 [55.56]	135 [45.00]	248 [41.33]
Once or twice	38 [38.00]	41 [37.27]	21 [23.33]	100 [33.33]	38 [33.04]	25 [26.32]	18 [20.00]	81 [27.00]	181 [30.17]
More often	30 [30.00]	29 [26.36]	28 [31.11]	87 [29.00]	41 [35.65]	21 [22.11]	22 [24.44]	84 [28.00]	171 [28.50]
N	100	110	90	300	115	95	90	300	600

Figures given in brackets indicate percentage.

respondents admitted that their husbands never talked about family planning measures. It was reported high in Pithoragarh and Udhamsingh Nagar (Table 28).

The respondents were asked regarding discussion with their husbands about number of children. About 19 per cent respondents admitted that they discussed it with their husbands. It was found more pronouncing in Azamgarh (21.0 per cent) and Dehradun (21.74 per cent). Only 10 per cent respondents in Jhansi accepted that they discussed with their husbands regarding number of children (Table 29).

The respondents were asked about their desire for children. Most of the respondents were in favour of one child. Interestingly, the desire for girl children was also quite high since 60 per cent women were found interested in having at least one girl child (Table 30).

The respondents were asked whether child or women is anemic or malnourished. About 31 per cent respondents admitted that either mother or child is anemic or malnourished. It was found more pronouncing in Jhansi (57.27 per cent) followed by Azamgarh (38.0 per cent). However, it was reported least in Dehradun (12.17 per cent). The proportion of respondents stating that mother or child is anemic has been recorded low in Uttaranchal as compared to Uttar Pradesh (Table 31).

Overall, fertility rate has been reported to be low. However, cases of infant mortality are found to be significant. The proportion of live births was significantly high in the surveyed areas. On an average 3.62 children per women was reported the partility (Table 32).

CONTRACEPTION

The use of contraceptives is shown in Table 33. Overall, 64.5 per cent women in Uttar Pradesh and 65.60 per cent women in Uttaranchal were found aware about contraceptives. Against it, more than one third women have ever used contraceptives. The awareness regarding injections, male sterilization, pills, loops/copper T, female sterilization, and rhythm or periodic abstinence has been reported to be significant. However, ever use method has been reported to

Table 29
Whether You Discuss with Your Husband Regarding Number of Children

	Uttar Pradesh				*Uttaranchal*				*Total*
	Azamgarh	*Jhansi*	*Sitapur*	*Sub-total*	*Dehradun*	*Pithora-garh*	*Udham Singh Nagar*	*Sub-total*	
Yes	21 [21.00]	11 [10.00]	19 [21.11]	51 [17.00]	25 [21.74]	20 [21.05]	18 [20.00]	63 [21.00]	114 [19.00]
No	79 [79.00]	99 [90.00]	71 [78.88]	249 [83.00]	90 [78.26]	75 [78.95]	72 [80.00]	237 [79.00]	486 [81.00]
N	100	110	90	300	115	95	90	300	600

Figures given in brackets indicate percentage.

Table 30
How Many Children Would You Like

		Uttar Pradesh				*Uttaranchal*				*Total*
		Azamgarh	*Jhansi*	*Sitapur*	*Sub-total*	*Dehradun garh*	*Pithora-Nagar*	*Udham Singh total*	*Sub-*	
Boys	1	35 [35.00]	36 [32.72]	20 [22.22]	91 [30.33]	80 [69.56]	29 [30.52]	20 [30.52]	129 [43.00]	220 [36.67]
	2	31 [31.00]	40 [36.36]	49 [54.44]	120 [40.00]	31 [26.95]	63 [66.31]	63 [66.31]	118 [39.33]	238 [39.67]
	3	24 [24.00]	14 [12.72]	14 [15.55]	52 [17.33]	4 [3.47]	3 [3.15]	3 [3.15]	37 [12.33]	89 [14.83]
	More than four	10 [10.00]	20 [18.18]	7 [7.77]	37 [12.33]	-	43 [45.26]	43 [45.26]	59 [19.67]	96 [16.00]
Girls	1	47 [47.00]	55 [50.00]	54 [60.00]	156 [52.00]	95 [82.60]	49 [51.57]	49 [51.57]	206 [68.67]	362 [60.33]
	2	24 [24.00]	34 [30.90]	36 [40.00]	94 [31.33]	20 [17.39]	3 [3.15]	3 [3.15]	40 [13.33]	134 [22.33]
	3	20 [20.00]	9 [8.18]	-	29 [9.67]	-	-	-	8 [2.67]	37 [6.17]
	More than four	9 [9.00]	12 [10.90]	-	21 [7.00]	-	-	-	3 [1.00]	24 [4.00]
	N	100	110	90	300	115	95	90	300	600

Figures given in brackets indicate percentage.

Table 31
Whether Child/Mother is Anemic

	Uttar Pradesh				*Uttaranchal*				*Total*
	Azamgarh	*Jhansi*	*Sitapur*	*Sub-total*	*Dehradun*	*Pithora-garh*	*Udham Singh Nagar*	*Sub-total*	
Yes	38 [38.00]	63 [57.27]	23 [25.55]	124 [41.33]	14 [12.17]	25 [26.31]	21 [23.33]	60 [20.00]	184 [30.66]
No	62 [62 00]	47 [42.72]	67 [74.44]	176 [58.66]	101 [87.82]	70 [73.68]	69 [76.66]	240 [80.00]	416 [69.33]
N	100	110	90	300	115	95	90	300	600

Figures given in brackets indicate percentage.

Table 32
Number of Alive/Dead Children Ever Born and Fertility Rate

	Uttar Pradesh				*Uttaranchal*				*Total*
		Azamgarh	*Jhansi*	*Sitapur*	*Sub-total*	*Dehradun*	*Pithora-garh*	*Udham Singh Nagar*	*Sub-total*
Alive	361 [4.20]	390 [3.98]	325 [4.11]	1076 [4.09]	397 [3.85]	329 [3.92]	333 [4.11]	1059 [3.95]	2135 [4.02]
Family	86	98	79	263	103	84	81	268	531
Dead	19 [1.27]	28 [1.65]	20 [1.67]	67 [1.52]	29 [1.38]	20 [1.11]	26 [1.73]	75 [1.39]	142 [1.49]
Family	15	17	12	44	21	18	15	54	98
Total Fertility Rate	3.76	3.63	3.79	3.72	3.44	3.42	3.74	3.52	3.62

Figures given in brackets indicate percentage.

Table 33
Use of Contraceptives

	Uttar Pradesh			*Uttaranchal*		
	Have you ever heard	*Have you ever Used*	*N*	*Have you ever heard*	*Have you ever Used*	*N*
Pills	167 [62.78]	99 [37.22]	266	257 [57.24]	192 [42.76]	449
Loops/Copper T	250 [63.45]	144 [36.55]	394	265 [68.30]	123 [31.70]	388
Injections	195 [87.17]	29 [12.83]	226	172 [71.67]	68 [28.33]	240
Condom	271 [53.14]	239 [46.86]	510	297 [56.90]	225 [43.10]	522
Female Sterilization	237 [56.83]	180 [43.17]	417	300 [63.16]	175 [36.84]	475
Male Sterilization	202 [94.39]	12 [5.61]	214	275 [91.97]	24 [8.03]	299
Rhythm or periodic abstinence	45 [64.29]	25 [35.71]	70	178 [79.82]	45 [20.18]	223
Withdrawal	176 [59.26]	121 [40.74]	297	178 [53.29]	156 [46.71]	334
Total	1545 [64.54]	849 [35.46]	2394	1922 [65.60]	1008 [34.40]	2930

Figures given in brackets indicate percentage

be high in case of condoms, pills, loops/copper T and female sterilization (Tab.e 33).

Current use of family planning measures is shown in Table 34. Overall, 28.33 per cent women are using family planning method. It was reported high in Udhamsingh Nagar (45.56 per cent) followed by Pithoragarh (40.0 per cent) and Sitapur (24.24 per cent). Those who are using contraceptive currently said that they are using mainly condoms, pills and sterilization.

Most of the women who are currently using family planning methods are facing problems. It was reported to be high in Azamgarh, Sitapur, and Pithoragarh districts. The main problems in use of contraceptives are weight gain, white discharge, nausa/vomiting, headache, and irregular periods (Table 35).

The sources of contraceptives are shown in Table 36. Most of the women get contraceptives from sub centres, clinics, hospitals, and nursing homes. The private agencies like nursing homes, private doctors, field workers and community based organizations also provide contraceptives.

A large number of women who faced problems in use of contraceptives stopped using family planning methods. The main factors responsible for the stoppage were related to health problems, lack of sexual satisfaction, disliking the method and non-availability of method (Table 37).

Education wise drop in use of family planning method is shown in Table 38. Those who are educated dropped the use of family planning methods as they do not suit them; however, it is difficult to understand the negative implications of contraceptives to illiterate women.

Age wise drop in use of family planning method is shown in Table 39. Most of the young women continued the use of family planning methods while aged women dropped the inuse variations in age across districts and states as far as dropout rates are concerned did exist.

Satisfaction regarding health services is shown in Table 40. In the state of Uttar Pradesh, most women were satisfied with the services of immunization, vaccination; medical treatment, institutional delivery, and health checkup, however, the service

Table 34
Currently Use of Contraceptives

	Uttar Pradesh				*Uttaranchal*				*Total*
	Azamgarh	*Jhansi*	*Sitapur*	*Sub-total*	*Dehradun*	*Pithora-garh*	*Udham Singh Nagar*	*Sub-total*	
Yes	18 [18.00]	20 [18.18]	22 [24.44]	60 [20.00]	31 [26.96]	38 [40.00]	41 [45.56]	110 [36.67]	170 [28.33]
No	82 [82.00]	90 [81.82]	68 [75.56]	240 [80.00]	84 [73.04]	57 [60.00]	49 [54.44]	190 [36.33]	430 [71.67]
N	100	110	90	300	115	95	90	300	600
If Yes									
Pills	8 [44.44]	10 [50.00]	5 [22.73]	23 [38.33]	15 [48.39]	17 [44.74]	23 [56.10]	55 [50.00]	78 [45.88]
Loops/Copper T	2 [11.11]	-	3 [13.64]	5 [8.33]	3 [9.68]	1 [2.63]	4 [9.76]	8 [7.27]	13 [7.65]
Injections	1 [5.56]	-	-	1 [1.67]	-	-	2 [4.88]	2 [1.82]	3 [1.76]
Condom	3 [16.67]	5 [25.00]	6 [27.27]	14 [23.33]	8 [25.81]	9 [23.68]	8 [19.51]	25 [22.73]	39 [22.94]
Female Sterilization	4 [22.22]	2 [10.00]	7 [31.82]	13 [21.67]	4 [12.90]	6 [15.97]	4 [9.76]	14 [12.73]	27 [15.88]
Male Sterilization	-	-	-	-	-	-	-	-	-
Rhythm or periodic abstinence	-	-	1 [4.55]	1 [1.67]	1 [3.23]	3 [7.89]	-	4 [3.64]	5 [2.94]
Withdrawal	-	2 [10.00]	-	2 [3.33]	-	2 [5.26]	-	2 [1.82]	4 [2.35]
Pills	-	-	-	-	-	-	-	-	-
N	18	20	22	60	31	38	41	110	170

Figures given in brackets indicate percentage.

Table 35
Problems in Use of Contraceptives

	Uttar Pradesh				*Uttaranchal*				*Total*
	Azamgarh	*Jhansi*	*Sitapur*	*Sub-total*	*Dehradun*	*Pithora-garh*	*Udham Singh Nagar*	*Sub-total*	
Yes	49 [49.00]	44 [40.00]	41 [45.56]	134 [44.67]	11 [9.57]	40 [42.11]	30 [33.33]	81 [27.00]	215 [35.83]
No	51 [51.00]	66 [60.00]	49 [54.44]	166 [55.33]	104 [90.43]	55 [57.89]	60 [66.67]	219 [77.00]	385 [64.17]
N	100	110	90	300	115	95	90	300	600
If Yes									
Cramps	5 [10.20]	-	-	5 [3.73]	-	-	-	-	5 [2.33]
Weight Gain	6 [12.24]	3 [6.82]	2 [4.88]	11 [8.21]	4 [36.36]	3 [7.50]	6 [20.00]	13 [16.45]	24 [11.16]
Dizzying	-	-	2 [4.88]	2 [1.49]	-	-	-	-	2 [0.93]
Body ache	4 [8.16]	5 [11.36]	3 [7.32]	12 [8.96]	1 [9.09]	4 [10.00]	5 [16.67]	10 [12.35]	22 [10.23]
Spotting/Bleeding	-	-	-	-	-	3 [7.50]	2 [6.67]	5 [6.17]	5 [2.33]
White discharge	2 [4.08]	7 [15.91]	8 [19.51]	17 [12.69]	-	6 [15.00]	3 [10.00]	9 [11.11]	26 [12.09]
Breast tenderness	-	-	-	-	-	-	-	-	-
Nausea/Vomiting	5 [10.20]	-	-	5 [3.73]	6 [54.55]	8 [20.00]	7 [23.33]	21 [25.93]	26 [12.09]
Cancer	-	-	-	-	-	-	-	-	-
Allergy	3 [6.12]	4 [9.09]	6 [14.63]	13 [9.70]	-	6 [15.00]	-	6 [7.41]	19 [8.84]
Headache	2 [4.08]	9 [20.45]	15 [36.59]	26 [19.40]	-	3 [7.50]	2 [6.67]	5 [6.17]	31 [14.42]
Irregular periods	7 [14.29]	10 [22.73]	2 [4.88]	19 [14.18]	-	5 [12.50]	4 [13.33]	9 [11.11]	28 [13.02]
Others	15 [30.61]	6 [13.64]	3 [7.32]	24 [17.91]	-	2 [5.00]	1 [3.33]	3 [3.70]	27 [12.56]
N	49	44	41	134	11	40	30	81	215

Figures given in brackets indicate percentage.

Table 36
Sources of Contraceptives

	Uttar Pradesh				*Uttaranchal*				*Total*
	Azamgarh	*Jhansi*	*Sitapur*	*Sub-total*	*Dehradun*	*Pithora-garh*	*Udham Singh Nagar*	*Sub-total*	
NGO	-	-	2 [9.09]	2 [3.33]	-	-	2 [4.88]	2 [1.82]	4 [2.35]
Panchayat	-	-	-	-	-	-	-	-	-
Hospital	2 [11.11]	-	1 [4.55]	3 [5.00]	3 [9.68]	3 [7.89]	8 [19.51]	14 [12.73]	17 [10.00]
Clinic	3 [16.67]	1 [5.00]	3 [13.64]	7 [11.67]	4 [12.90]	4 [10.53]	4 [9.76]	12 [10.91]	19 [11.18]
Private Hospital	4 [22.22]		2 [9.09]	6 [10.00]	2 [6.45]	-	5 [12.20]	7 [6.36]	13 [7.65]
Nursing Home	3 [16.67]	4 [20.00]	4 [18.18]	11 [18.33]	5 [16.13]	6 [15.79]	10 [24.39]	21 [19.09]	32 [18.82]
Sub-centre	2 [11.11]	3 [15.00]	3 [13.64]	8 [13.33]	4 [12.90]	5 [13.16]	6 [14.63]	15 [13.64]	23 [13.53]
Pharmacy	3 [16.67]	10 [50.00]	7 [31.82]	20 [33.33]	10 [32.26]	15 [39.47]	6 [14.63]	31 [28.18]	51 [30.00]
Private doctors	1 [5.56]	2 [10.00]		3 [5.00]	3 [9.68]	3 [7.89]	-	6 [5.45]	9 [5.29]
Mobile clinic	-	-	-	-	-	-	-	-	-
Field Workers	-	-	-	-	-	2 [5.26]	-	-	2 [1.18]
N	18	20	22	60	31	38	41	110	170

Table 37
Whether You Stopped Using Family Planning Methods

	Uttar Pradesh				*Uttaranchal*				*Total*
	Azamgarh	*Jhansi*	*Sitapur*	*Sub-total*	*Dehradun*	*Pithora-garh*	*Udham Singh Nagar*	*Sub-total*	
Yes	6 [12.24]	5 [11.36]	3 [7.32]	14 [10.45]	2 [18.18]	5 [12.50]	4 [13.33]	11 [13.58]	25 [11.63]
No	43 [87.76]	39 [88.64]	38 [92.68]	120 [89.25]	9 [81.82]	35 [87.50]	26 [86.67]	70 [86.42]	190 [88.37]
N	49	44	41	134	11	40	30	81	215
If Yes									
Method failed	-	-	-	-	-	-	-	-	-
Lack of sexual satisfaction	-	-	-	-	-	-	-	-	-
Created health problems	3 [50.00]	4 [80.00]	2 [66.67]	9 [64.29]	2 [100.00]	3 [60.00]	2 [50.00]	7 [63.64]	16 [64.00]
Inconvenient to use	-	-	-	-	-	-	-	-	-
Not easily available	-	-	-	-	-	-	-	-	-
Did not like the method	1 [16.67]	-	-	1 [7.14]	-	-	-	-	-
Wanted to have a child	2 [33.33]	1 [20.00]	-	3 [21.43]	-	1 [20.00]	1 [25.00]	2 [18.18]	5 [20.00]
Others	-	-	1 [33.33]	1 [7.14]	-	1 [20.00]	1 [25.00]	2 [18.18]	3 [12.00]
N	6	5	3	14	2	5	4	11	25

Figures given in brackets indicate percentage.

Table 38
Education wise Drop in Use of Family Planning Method

	Uttar Pradesh	Uttaranchal	Total
Illiterate	-	-	-
Literate	-	1 [9.09]	1 [4.00]
Up to Primary	2 [14.29]	1 [9.09]	3 [12.00]
Jr. High School	5 [35.71]	2 [18.18]	7 [28.00]
Intermediate	2 [14.29]	3 [27.27]	5 [20.00]
Graduate	3 [21.43]	3 [27.27]	6 [24.00]
Post Graduate	2 [14.29]	1 [9.09]	3 [12.00]
Others	-	-	-
N	14	11	25

Figures given in brackets indicate percentage.

Table 39
Age wise Drop in Use of Family Planning Method

	Uttar Pradesh	Uttaranchal	Total
Less then 18 years	-	-	-
19-25 years	3 [21.43]	2 [18.18]	5 [20.00]
26-35 years	8 [57.14]	6 [54.55]	14 [56.00]
36-45 years	3 [21.43]	2 [18.18]	5 [20.00]
46-55 years	-	-	-
55 to above	-	-	-
N	14	11	25

Figures given in brackets indicate percentage.

of HIV/AIDS prevention, postnatal care, nutrition supply, referral services etc. are found to be poor. Similarly, in the state of Uttaranchal, the services of immunization, vaccination, health checkup, medical treatment, referral services, and prenatal care were found quite satisfactory, however, the services of nutrition supply, postnatal care, institutional delivery etc. were found poor.

IMMUNIZATION AND VACCINATION

The women were asked whether they received vaccination card. About three fourth respondents reported that they received vaccination card. It was reported high in Jhansi followed by Dehradun. However, it was reported as low as 57.77 per cent in Sitapur (Table 41).

Table 40
Satisfaction Regarding Health Services

	Uttar Pradesh					*Uttaranchal*				
	Very Satisfactory	*Somewhat Satisfactory*	*Satisfactory*	*Not Satisfactory*	*N*	*Very Satisfactory*	*Somewhat Satisfactory*	*Satisfactory*	*Not Satisfactory*	*N*
Immunization	164 [54.67]	144 [38.00]	17 [5.67]	5 [1.67]	300	147 [49.00]	110 [36.67]	40 [13.33]	3 [1.00]	300
Vaccination	137 [45.67]	133 [44.33]	22 [7.33]	8 [2.67]	300	148 [49.33]	98 [32.67]	49 [16.33]	5 [1.67]	300
Health checkup	114 [38.00]	139 [46.33]	30 [10.00]	17 [5.67]	300	128 [42.67]	114 [38.00]	45 [15.00]	13 [4.33]	300
Medical Treatment	92 [30.67]	155 [51.67]	38 [12.67]	15 [5.00]	300	110 [36.67]	139 [46.33]	31 [10.33]	20 [6.67]	300
Referral services	80 [26.67]	80 [26.67]	23 [7.67]	117 [39.00]	300	139 [46.33]	108 [36.00]	36 [12.00]	17 [5.67]	300
Nutrition supply	90 [30.00]	104 [34.67]	53 [17.67]	53 [17.67]	300	91 [30.33]	88 [29.33]	58 [19.33]	63 [21.00]	300
Prenatal care	72 [24.00]	135 [45.00]	53 [17.67]	40 [13.33]	300	121 [40.33]	104 [34.67]	59 [19.67]	16 [5.33]	300
Postnatal care	49 [16.33]	152 [50.67]	40 [13.33]	59 [19.67]	300	121 [40.33]	112 [37.33]	55 [18.33]	12 [4.00]	300
Institutional delivery of pregnancy	69 [23.00]	189 [63.00]	18 [6.00]	24 [8.00]	300	97 [32.33]	110 [36.67]	48 [16.00]	45 [15.00]	300
STD/HIV/AIDS prevention	74 [24.67]	14 [4.67]	100 [33.33]	112 [37.33]	300	4 [1.33]	80 [26.67]	52 [17.33]	164 [54.67]	300
Others	70 [23.33]	115 [38.33]	80 [26.67]	35 [11.67]	300	90 [30.00]	100 [33.33]	25 [8.33]	85 [28.33]	300
Total	1011 [30.64]	1330 [40.30]	474 [14.36]	485 [14.70]	3300	1196 [36.24]	1163 [35.24]	498 [15.09]	443 [13.42]	3300

Figures given in brackets indicate percentage

Table 41
Did You Have a Vaccination Card

	Uttar Pradesh				*Uttaranchal*				*Total*
	Azamgarh	*Jhansi*	*Sitapur*	*Sub-total*	*Dehradun*	*Pithora-garh*	*Udham Singh Nagar*	*Sub-total*	
Yes	75 [75.00]	98 [89.09]	52 [57.77]	255 [75.00]	92 [80.00]	58 [61.05]	64 [71.11]	214 [71.33]	439 [73.16]
No	25 [25.00]	12 [10.90]	38 [42.22]	75 [25.00]	23 [20.00]	37 [38.94]	26 [28.88]	86 [28.66]	161 [26.83]
N	100	110	90	300	115	95	90	300	600

Figures given in brackets indicate percentage.

Table 42
Do You Received Vaccination for Your Children

	Uttar Pradesh					*Uttaranchal*				
	Boys		*Girls*		*N*	*Boys*		*Girls*		*N*
	Yes	*No*	*Yes*	*No*		*Yes*	*No*	*Yes*	*No*	
BCG	258 [86.00]	42 [14.00]	227 [75.66]	73 [24.33]	300	265 [88.33]	35 [11.66]	215 [71.66]	85 [28.33]	300
Polio	251 [83.66]	49 [16.33]	272 [90.66]	28 [9.33]	300	245 [81.66]	55 [18.33]	280 [93.33]	20 [6.66]	300
DPT	273 [91.00]	27 [9.00]	245 [81.66]	55 [18.33]	300	256 [85.33]	44 [14.66]	230 [76.66]	70 [23.33]	300
Hepatitis B/C	173 [57.66]	127 [42.33]	90 [30.00]	210 [70.00]	300	172 [57.33]	128 [42.66]	145 [48.33]	155 [51.66]	300
Measles	274 [91.33]	26 [8.66]	242 [80.66]	58 [19.33]	300	252 [84.00]	48 [16.00]	233 [77.66]	67 [22.33]	300
Chickenpox	258 [86.00]	42 [14.00]	236 [78.66]	64 [21.33]	300	175 [58.33]	125 [41.66]	152 [50.66]	148 [49.33]	300
N	1487 [82.61]	313 [17.38]	1312 [72.88]	488 [27.11]	1800	1365 [75.83]	435 [24.16]	1155 [64.16]	645 [35.83]	1800

Figures given in brackets indicate percentage.

The women were further asked about receiving of vaccination to their children. Overall, vaccination against deadly diseases has been reported to be higher among male children as compared to girl children. Thus, it is clear that girl children are being discriminated even in vaccination against deadly diseases. Only 82.61 per cent and 75.83 per cent boys in Uttar Pradesh and Uttaranchal get vaccination against deadly diseases as against 72.88 per cent and 64.16 per cent girls in these states. Vaccination rate has been reported slightly higher in Uttar Pradesh as compared to Uttaranchal (Table 42).

Place of vaccination is given in Table 43. In most of the cases, vaccinations were given at community centre level, house level, and PHC's/CHC's level. Even, a large number of women received vaccination to their children at private nursing home hospitals. In most of the cases multiple sources of vaccination were reported.

About two fifth respondents also revealed that they did seek advice for treatment for diarrhoea to their children. It was reported high in Sitapur and Pithoragarh districts. Most of them, received treatment at government hospital, PHC's/CHC's however, community based organizations also provided facilities for treatment of diarrhoea (Table 44).

DAUGHTER DISADVANTAGES

In this part of chapter, an attempt has been made to examine the daughter disadvantages by analyzing view perception of women. Only 10.50 per cent women were found in favour of gender testing of baby in wombs. It was reported to be high in Azamgarh (24.0 per cent) followed by Pithoragarh (18.95 per cent). Most of them were against aminiosyn-thesis to examine the sex of baby in womb (Table 45).

The respondents were further asked about their experience of gender testing of baby in womb. Only 2.17 per cent of them had its experience. It was found more pronouncing in Azamgarh and Pithoragarh districts (Table 46).

Only three women experienced abortion of pregnancy due to gender testing of baby. It was reported high in Azamgarh, Sitapur and Pithoragarh districts (Table 47). All such

Table 43
Place of Vaccinations

	Uttar Pradesh				*Uttaranchal*				*Total*
	Azamgarh	*Jhansi*	*Sitapur*	*Sub-total*	*Dehradun*	*Pithora-garh*	*Udham Singh Nagar*	*Sub-total*	
Home	40 [40.00]	65 [59.09]	75 [83.33]	180 [60.00]	100 [86.95]	45 [47.36]	80 [88.88]	225 [75.00]	405 [67.50]
Community centre	56 [56.00]	75 [68.18]	90 [100.00]	221 [73.67]	115 [100.00]	95 [100.00]	76 [84.44]	286 [95.33]	507 [84.50]
Village/Ward Level	12 [12.00]	25 [22.72]	7 [7.77]	44 [14.67]	45 [39.13]	15 [15.78]	30 [33.33]	90 [30.00]	134 [22.33]
Sub centre	3 [3.00]	45 [40.90]	20 [22.22]	68 [22.67]	26 [22.60]	56 [58.94]	12 [13.33]	94 [31.33]	162 [27.00]
PHC/CHC	70 [70.00]	100 [90.90]	88 [97.77]	258 [86.00]	100 [86.95]	75 [78.94]	85 [94.44]	260 [86.66]	518 [86.33]
Private Nursing Home/Hospital	100 [100.00]	95 [86.36]	82 [91.11]	277 [92.33]	115 [1.00]	90 [94.73]	76 [84.44]	281 [93.66]	558 [93.00]
N	100	110	90	300	115	95	90	300	600

Figures given in brackets indicate percentage.

Table 44
Did You Seek Advice or Treatment for Diarrhoea

	Uttar Pradesh				*Uttaranchal*				*Total*
	Azamgarh	*Jhansi*	*Sitapur*	*Sub-total*	*Dehradun*	*Pithora-garh*	*Udham Singh Nagar*	*Sub-total*	
Yes	37 [37.00]	28 [25.45]	49 [54.44]	114 [38.00]	50 [43.48]	47 [49.47]	30 [33.33]	127 [42.33]	241 [40.17]
No	63 [63.00]	82 [74.55]	41 [44.56]	186 [62.00]	65 [56.52]	48 [50.53]	60 [66.67]	173 [57.67]	359 [59.83]
N	100	110	90	300	115	95	90	300	600
If Yes where									
Government Hospital	33 [89.19]	7 [25.00]	28 [57.14]	68 [59.65]	35 [70.00]	27 [57.45]	24 [80.00]	86 [67.72]	154 [63.90]
PHC/CHC	14 [37.84]	20 [71.43]	27 [55.10]	61 [54.51]	31 [62.00]	29 [61.70]	21 [70.00]	81 [63.78]	142 [58.92]
Sub-centre	2 [5.41]	27 [96.43]	6 [12.24]	35 [30.70]	3 [6.00]	-	8 [26.67]	11 [8.66]	46 [19.09]
Mobile Clinic	-	3 [10.71]	2 [4.08]	5 [4.39]	15 [30.00]	16 [34.04]	4 [13.33]	35 [27.56]	40 [16.60]
Village Health Guide	3 [8.11]	6 [21.43]	6 [12.24]	15 [13.16]	-	12 [25.53]	8 [26.67]	20 [15.75]	35 [14.52]
ANM/LHV	4 [10.81]	20 [71.43]	8 [16.33]	32 [28.07]	19 [38.00]	4 [8.51]	7 [23.33]	30 [23.62]	62 [25.73]
NGO	-	8 [28.57]	2 [4.08]	10 [8.77]	30 [60.00]	21 [44.68]	5 [16.67]	56 [44.09]	66 [27.39]
Panchayat	-	-	-	-	-	-	-	-	-
Others	35 [94.59]	4 [14.29]	-	39 [34.21]	45 [90.00]	40 [85.11]	12 [40.00]	97 [76.38]	136 [56.43]
N	37	28	49	114	50	47	30	127	241

Figures given in brackets indicate percentage.

Table 45
Do You Approve Gender Testing of Baby in Womb

	Uttar Pradesh				*Uttaranchal*				*Total*
	Azamgarh	*Jhansi*	*Sitapur*	*Sub-total*	*Dehradun*	*Pithora-garh*	*Udham Singh Nagar*	*Sub-total*	
Yes	24 [24.00]	-	11 [12.22]	35 [11.67]	-	18 [18.95]	10 [11.11]	28 [9.33]	63 [10.50]
No	76 [76.00]	110 [100.00]	79 [87.78]	265 [87.78]	115 [100.00]	77 [81.05]	80 [88.89]	272 [90.67]	537 [89.50]
N	100	110	90	300	115	95	90	300	600

Figures given in brackets indicate percentage.

Table 46
Whether Your Family Experienced Gender Testing of a Baby in Womb

	Uttar Pradesh				*Uttaranchal*				*Total*
	Azamgarh	*Jhansi*	*Sitapur*	*Sub-total*	*Dehradun*	*Pithora-garh*	*Udham Singh Nagar*	*Sub-total*	
Yes	4 [4.00]	-	2 [2.22]	6 [2.00]	-	4 [4.21]	3 [3.33]	7 [2.33]	13 [2 17]
No	70 [70.00]	90 [81.82]	74 [82.22]	234 [78.00]	97 [84.35]	63 [66.32]	60 [66.67]	220 [73.33]	454 [75.67]
Can not say	26 [26.00]	20 [18.18]	14 [15.56]	60 [20.00]	18 [15.65]	28 [29.47]	27 [30.00]	72 [24.33]	133 [22.17]
N	100	110	90	300	115	95	90	300	600

Figures given in brackets indicate percentage.

Table 47
Whether You Experienced Abortion of Pregnancy

	Uttar Pradesh				*Uttaranchal*				*Total*
	Azamgarh	*Jhansi*	*Sitapur*	*Sub-total*	*Dehradun*	*Pithora-garh*	*Udham Singh Nagar*	*Sub-total*	
Yes	-	-	1 [50.00]	1 [16.67]	-	1 [25.00]	1 [33.33]	2 [28.57]	3 [23.08]
No	4100.00	-	1 [50.00]	5 [83.33]	-	3 [75.00]	2 [66.67]	5 [71.43]	10 [76.92]
N	4	-	2	6	-	4	3	7	13

Figures given in brackets indicate percentage.

Table 48
Sex of Aborted Child

	Uttar Pradesh				*Uttaranchal*				*Total*
	Azamgarh	*Jhansi*	*Sitapur*	*Sub-total*	*Dehradun*	*Pithora-garh*	*Udham Singh Nagar*	*Sub-total*	
Male	-	-	-	-	-	1 [25.00]	-	1 [14.29]	1 [7.69]
Female	4100.00	-	2 [100.00]	6 [100.00]	-	3 [75.00]	3 [100.00]	6 [85.71]	12 [92.31]
N	4	-	2	6	-	4	3	7	13

Figures given in brackets indicate percentage.

Table 49
Do you Experience Discrimination of Girl Children in Proper Care

	Uttar Pradesh				*Uttaranchal*				*Total*
	Azamgarh	*Jhansi*	*Sitapur*	*Sub-total*	*Dehradun*	*Pithora-garh*	*Udham Singh Nagar*	*Sub-total*	
Yes	51 [51.00]	73 [66.36]	35 [38.88]	159 [53.00]	22 [19.13]	54 [56.84]	30 [33.33]	106 [35.33]	265 [44.16]
No	19 [19.00]	24 [21.81]	26 [28.88]	69 [23.00]	79 [68.69]	25 [26.31]	60 [66.66]	164 [54.66]	233 [38.83]
Can not say	12 [12.00]	13 [11.81]	29 [32.22]	54 [18.00]	14 [12.17]	16 [16.84]	-	30 [10.00]	74 [14.00]
N	100	110	90	300	115	95	90	300	600
If Yes, in what form									
Care	39 [76.47]	47 [64.38]	33 [94.28]	119 [74.84]	16 [72.72]	47 [87.03]	25 [83.33]	88 [83.01]	207 [78.11]
Nutrition and food intakes	34 [66.66]	30 [41.09]	27 [77.14]	83 [52.20]	15 [68.18]	41 [75.92]	30 [100.00]	86 [81.13]	169 [63.77]
Health checkup	24 [47.05]	68 [93.15]	19 [54.28]	111 [68.91]	12 [54.54]	24 [44.44]	15 [50.00]	51 [48.11]	162 [61.13]
Medical treatment	39 [76.47]	48 [65.75]	18 [51.42]	105 [66.03]	2 [9.09]	15 [27.77]	28 [93.33]	45 [42.45]	150 [56.60]
Preference of health centres	30 [58.82]	6 [8.21]	23 [65.71]	59 [37.10]	10 [45.45]	27 [50.00]	21 [70.00]	58 [54.71]	117 [44.15]
Schooling	49 [96.07]	66 [90.41]	30 [85.71]	145 [91.19]	20 [90.90]	37 [68.51]	24 [80.00]	81 [76.41]	226 [85.28]
Marriage	10 [19.60]	63 [86.30]	25 [71.42]	98 [61.13]	6 [27.27]	10 [18.51]	25 [83.33]	41 [38.67]	139 [52.45]
Others	30 [58.82]	44 [60.27]	4 [11.42]	78 [49.05]	15 [68.18]	12 [22.22]	15 [50.00]	42 [39.62]	120 [45.28]
N	51	73	35	159	22	54	30	106	265

Figures given in brackets indicate percentage.

respondents stated that the sex of baby was female except one case of male in Pithoragarh district (Table 48).

The women were asked regarding gender discrimination in care, protection and treatment. About two fifth respondents revealed that girls are being discriminated in care, heath care, treatment and education. It was found more pronouncing in Jhansi (66.36 per cent) followed by Pithoragarh (56.84 per cent) and Azamgarh (51.00 per cent). The discrimination is reported high in case of schooling (85.28 per cent), care (78.1 per cent), nutrition and food (63.77 per cent), and health checkup (61.13 per cent). Even the girls are being discriminated in their marriage since girls are married off early as compared to boys (Table 49).

About half of the respondents reported that they have the experience of early marriage of daughters. It was reported high in Jhansi (84.54 per cent) followed by Azamgarh (41.0 per cent) and Dehradun (40.86 per cent). In most of the cases they experienced early marriage of their daughters, (67.02 per cent) self (58.86 per cent) and their sisters (Table 50).

The respondents were further asked about the factors for early marriage. Prevailing customs, value, traditions, avoidance of dowry, and economic hardship were reported the important factors responsible for early marriage of girls (Table 51).

Overall, the analysis shows that the health status of women was somewhat satisfactory in the surveyed areas. Health care services were available to most of the women; however, early marriage of women was found an alarming trend. Girls were being still discriminated on several fronts. The boys were getting better opportunities for care, education, health care and protection while girls disadvantages were reported in majority of the cases. Variations across the districts and states were found as far as health care services were concerned.

Table 50

Whether your Family Experience any Marriage Before Attaining the Age of 18 years

	Uttar Pradesh				*Uttaranchal*				*Total*
	Azamgarh	*Jhansi*	*Sitapur*	*Sub-total*	*Dehradun*	*Pithora-garh*	*Udham Singh Nagar*	*Sub-total*	
Yes	41 [41.00]	93 [84.54]	34 [37.77]	168 [56.00]	47 [40.86]	37 [38.94]	30 [33.33]	114 [38.00]	282 [47.00]
No	29 [29.00]	13 [11.81]	39 [43.33]	81 [27.00]	26 [22.60]	33 [34.73]	40 [44.44]	99 [33.00]	180 [30.00]
Cannot say	30 [30.00]	4 [3.63]	17 [18.88]	51 [17.00]	42 [36.52]	25 [26.31]	20 [22.22]	87 [29.00]	138 [23.00]
N	100	110	90	300	115	95	90	300	600
If Yes									
Daughter	41 [100.00]	60 [64.51]	34 [100.00]	136 [80.95]	25 [53.19]	13 [35.13]	15 [50.00]	53 [46.49]	189 [67.02]
Self	40 [97.56]	56 [60.21]	30 [88.23]	126 [75.00]	15 [31.91]	8 [21.62]	17 [56.66]	40 [35.08]	166 [58.86]
Son	13 [31.70]	57 [61.29]	14 [41.17]	84 [50.00]	5 [10.63]	4 [10.81]	9 [30.00]	18 [15.78]	102 [36.17]
Sister	19 [46.34]	80 [86.02]	7 [20.58]	106 [63.09]	10 [21.27]	5 [13.51]	18 [60.00]	33 [28.94]	139 [49.29]
Nice/nephew	24 [58.53]	10 [10.75]	11 [32.35]	45 [26.78]	35 [74.46]	25 [67.56]	20 [66.66]	80 [70.17]	125 [44.32]
Others	12 [29.26]	42 [45.16]	15 [44.11]	69 [41.07]	30 [63.82]	31 [83.78]	26 [86.66]	87 [76.31]	156 [55.31]
N	41	93	34	168	47	37	30	114	282

Figures given in brackets indicate percentage.

Table 51

What Were thc Reasons for Early Marriage

	Uttar Pradesh				*Uttranchal*				*Total*
	Azamgarh	*Jhansi*	*Sitapur*	*Sub-total*	*Dehradun*	*Pithora-garh*	*Udham Singh Nagar*	*Sub-total*	
Prevailing customs, value, traditions	30 [73.17]	76 [81.72]	31 [91.18]	137 [81.55]	40 [85.11]	32 [86.49]	19 [63.33]	91 [79.82]	228 [80.85]
Avoidance of dowry	15 [36.59]	90 [96.77]	30 [88.24]	135 [80.36]	41 [87.23]	31 [83.78]	24 [80.00]	96 [84.21]	231 [81.91]
Economic hardship	25 [60.98]	61 [65.59]	27 [79.41]	113 [67.26]	37 [78.72]	30 [81.08]	30 [100.00]	97 [85.09]	210 [74.47]
Care of siblings at home	18 [43.90]	51 [54.84]	26 [76.47]	95 [56.55]	25 [53.19]	18 [48.65]	24 [80.00]	67 [58.77]	162 [57.45]
Maintenance of home and cooking meal	21 [51.22]	36 [38.71]	24 [70.59]	81 [48.21]	30 [63.83]	24 [64.86]	15 [50.00]	69 [60.53]	150 [53.19]
Others	34 [82.93]	45 [48.39]	12 [35.29]	91 [54.17]	34 [72.34]	19 [51.35]	18 [60.00]	71 [62.28]	162 [57.45]
N	41	93	34	168	47	37	30	114	282

Figures given in brackets indicate percentage.

6

VIEWS OF OFFICIALS AND NON-OFFICIALS

Officials and non-officials were surveyed to examine their views related to health care services. Overall 156 officials and non-officials were contacted. Most of the officials belonged to ICDS Department, schools and health centres. The non-officials were mainly representatives of Panchayats and community based organizations (Table 1).

The location of such officials and non-officials is shown in Table 2. Majority of the respondents were from rural areas (55.13 per cent) while 44.87 per cent of them were from urban locations (Table 2).

The average distance of health centres and other important facilities is shown in Table 3. The average distance of railway station, bus station, inter-college and degree college has been reported to be greater while that of health centres 1 to 4 Km. It has been reported comparatively greater in Uttaranchal as compared to Uttar Pradesh due its hilly and tough terrain.

Main source of drinking water has been reported hand pump. However, it is not clear whether such hand-pumps are India Mark II which insure quality of drinking water. However, a substantial percentage get piped water supply.

Table 1
Category of Officials and Non-officials

	Uttar Pradesh				*Uttaranchal*				*Total*
	Azamgarh	*Jhansi*	*Sitapur*	*Sub-total*	*Dehradun*	*Pithora-garh*	*Udham Singh Nagar*	*Sub-total*	
Officials									
ICDS Department	4	4	4	12	4	4	4	12	24
Medical Doctor	4	4	4	12	4	4	4	12	24
Teachers	6	6	6	18	6	6	6	18	36
Total	14	14	14	42	14	14	14	42	84
Non-officials									
Panchayat members	3	3	3	9	3	3	3	9	18
NGO representative	4	4	4	12	4	4	4	12	24
Local leaders	5	5	5	15	5	5	5	15	30
Total	12	12	12	36	12	12	12	36	72

Table 2
Location of Area

	Uttar Pradesh			*Uttaranchal*			*Total*
	Officials	*Non-officials*	*Sub-total*	*Officials*	*Non-officials*	*Sub-Total*	
Urban	27 [64.29]	5 [13.89]	32 [41.03]	30 [71.43]	8 [22.22]	38 [48.72]	70 [44.87]
Rural	15 [35.71]	31 [86.11]	46 [58.97]	12 [28.57]	28 [77.78]	40 [51.28]	86 [55.13]
N	42	36	78	42	36	78	156

Figures given in brackets indicate percentage.

Table 3
Average Distance of Following Facilities (in Km.)

	Uttar Pradesh	*Uttaranchal*	*Average*
CHC	3.50	3.00	3.75
PHC	2.50	2.00	2.25
Sub centre	2.00	1.00	1.50
Public hospital	1.00	1.00	1.00
Pvt. Hospital	1.00	1.50	1.25
Nursing home	5.00	3.00	4.00
Medical shop	1.00	1.20	1.10
Primary school	0.50	0.50	0.50
Jr. high school	3.50	2.50	3.00
High school	4.50	6.50	5.50
Inter college	4.50	6.50	6.50
Degree college	10.00	10.00	10.00
Railway station	35.00	45.00	40.00
Bus station	10.00	32.00	21.00
Main pucca road	1.00	1.00	1.00

People also fetch drinking water from unsafe sources (Table 4).

The respondents were asked regarding the existence of sever lines in the surveyed areas. Only 18 per cent respondents reported in the affirmative. It was reported high in Uttaranchal as compared to Uttar Pradesh (Table 5).

About 19 per cent respondents reported that they have in their houses flush latrines to flush out human excreta. This was

Table 4
Main Source of Drinking Water

	Uttar Pradesh			Uttaranchal			Total
	Officials	Non-officials	Sub-total	Officials	Non-officials	Sub-Total	
Piped water	10 [23.81]	3 [8.33]	13 [16.67]	10 [23.81]	-	10 [12.82]	23 [14.74]
Handpump	32 [76.19]	33 [91.67]	65 [83.33]	25 [59.52]	24 [66.67]	49 [62.82]	114 [73.08]
Pond/lack	-	-	-	5 [11.90]	12 [33.33]	17 [21.79]	17 [10.90]
Spring water	-	-	-	-	-	-	-
Others	-	-	-	2 [4.76]	-	-	2 [1.28]
N	42	36	78	42	36	78	156

Figures given in brackets indicate percentage.

Table 5
Existence of Sever-line

	Uttar Pradesh			Uttaranchal			Total
	Officials	Non-officials	Sub-total	Officials	Non-officials	Sub-Total	
Yes	6 [14.29]	-	6 [7.69]	12 [28.57]	10 [27.78]	22 [28.21]	28 [17.95]
No	[85.71]	36 [100.00]	72 [92.31]	30 [71.43]	26 [72.22]	56 [71.79]	128 [82.05]
N	42	36	78	42	36	78	156

Figures given in brackets indicate percentage.

found more pronouncing in Uttaranchal as compared to Uttar Pradesh. About 80 per cent of them said that people defecate in open in the absence of sanitary toilets (Table 6).

About 20 per cent respondents reported that drainage facility is existing in their area. It was again reported high in Uttaranchal as compared to Uttar Pradesh (Table 7).

Respondents were asked regarding problem of sever chocking. Most of them reported that they never faced such problem however, 18 per cent respondents said that they face this problem occasionally while 15 per cent of them face it often (Table 8).

Table 6
Disposal of Human Excreta

	Uttar Pradesh			*Uttaranchal*			*Total*
	Officials	*Non-officials*	*Sub-total*	*Officials*	*Non-officials*	*Sub-Total*	
Flush latrine	5 [11.90]	9 [25.00]	14 [17.95]	10 [23.81]	6 [16.67]	16 [20.51]	30 [19.23]
Service latrine	2 [4.76]	-	2 [2.56]	-	-	-	4 [2.56]
Open defection	35 [83.33]	27 [75.00]	62 [79.49]	32 [76.19]	30 [83.33]	62 [79.29]	124 [79.49]
N	42	36	78	42	36	78	156

Figures given in brackets indicate percentage.

Table 7
Existence of Drainage System

	Uttar Pradesh			*Uttaranchal*			*Total*
	Officials	*Non-officials*	*Sub-total*	*Officials*	*Non-officials*	*Sub-Total*	
Yes	3 [7.14]	-	3 [3.85]	15 [35.71]	13 [36.11]	28 [35.90]	31 [19.87]
No	39 [92.86]	36 [100.00]	75 [76.15]	27 [64.29]	23 [63.89]	50 [64.10]	125 [80.13]
N	42	36	78	42	36	78	156

Figures given in brackets indicate percentage.

Table 8
Problem of Sewer Chocking

	Uttar Pradesh			*Uttaranchal*			*Total*
	Officials	*Non-officials*	*Sub-total*	*Officials*	*Non-officials*	*Sub-Total*	
Very often	-	-	-	-	-	-	-
Often	-	-	-	2 [16.67]	2 [20.00]	4 [18.18]	4 [14.89]
Occasionally	-	-	-	3 [25.00]	2 [20.00]	5 [22.73]	5 [17.86]
Never	6 [100.00]	-	6 [100.00]	7 [58.33]	6 [60.00]	13 [59.09]	19 [67.86]
N	6	-	6	12	10	22	28

Figures given in brackets indicate percentage.

Coupled with this problem water logging is more serious problem in U.P than the state of Uttaranchal. However, only a few respondents reported it occurring occasionally (Table 9).

Table 9
Problem of Water Logging

	Uttar Pradesh			*Uttaranchal*			*Total*
	Officials	*Non-officials*	*Sub-total*	*Officials*	*Non-officials*	*Sub-Total*	
Very often	3 [7.14]	-	3 [3.85]	-	1 [2.78]	1 [1.28]	4 [2.56]
Often	7 [16.67]	-	7 [8.97]	-	2 [5.56]	2 [2.56]	9 [5.77]
Occasionally	2[4.76]	8 [22.22]	10 [12.82]	7 [16.67]	5 [13.89]	12 [15.38]	22 [14.10]
Never	30 [71.43]	28 [77.78]	58 [74.36]	35 [83.33]	28 [77.78]	63 [80.77]	121 [77.56]
N	42	36	78	42	36	78	156

Figures given in brackets indicate percentage.

Table 10
How often Health Worker Visit in your Area

	Uttar Pradesh			*Uttaranchal*			*Total*
	Officials	*Non-officials*	*Sub-total*	*Officials*	*Non-officials*	*Sub-Total*	
Regularly	10 [23.81]	-	10 [12.82]	13 [30.95]	-	13 [16.67]	23 [14.74]
Sometimes	11 [26.19]	7 [19.44]	18 [23.08]	12 [28.57]	-	12 [15.38]	30 [19.23]
Occasionally	21 [50.00]	5 [13.89]	26 [33.33]	17 [40.48]	8 [22.22]	25 [32.05]	51 [32.69]
Never	-	24 [66.67]	24 [30.77]	-	28 [77.78]	28 [35.90]	52 [33.33]
N	42	36	78	42	36	78	156

Figures given in brackets indicate percentage.

Thus, the sanitation facilities in the surveyed areas are found be poor and wanting which offords the chances of water born diseases. Hence people face problems of poor health recovery. Visit by health workers is shown in Table 10. About one third respondents said that health workers never visit their areas. It was reported high in Uttaranchal as compared to Uttar Pradesh. About 15 per cent reported that health workers regularly visit their areas. About one third maintained that health workers visit their areas occasionally only.

About two fifth respondents stated that health camps are organized occasionally, however, about one fourth of them maintained that health camps are being organized very often (Table 11).

Table 11
Organization of Health Camps

	Uttar Pradesh			*Uttaranchal*			*Total*
	Officials	*Non-officials*	*Sub-total*	*Officials*	*Non-officials*	*Sub-Total*	
Very often	15 [35.71]	-	15 [19.23]	21 [50.00]	-	21 [26.92]	36 [23.08]
Often	10 [23.81]	-	10 [12.82]	9 [21.43]	1 [2.78]	10 [12.82]	20 [12.82]
Occasionally	17 [40.48]	19 [52.78]	36 [46.15]	12 [28.57]	15 [41.67]	27 [34.62]	63 [40.38]
Never	-	17 [47.22]	17 [21.79]	-	20 [55.56]	20 [25.64]	37 [23.72]
N	42	36	78	42	36	78	156

Figures given in brackets indicate percentage.

Table 12
Whether Special Drive for Vaccination and Immunization

	Uttar Pradesh			*Uttaranchal*			*Total*
	Officials	*Non-officials*	*Sub-total*	*Officials*	*Non-officials*	*Sub-Total*	
Yes	42 [100.00]	26 [72.22]	68 [87.18]	42 [100.00]	24 [66.67]	66 [84.62]	134 [84.90]
No	-	10 [27.78]	10 [12.82]	-	12 [33.33]	12 [15.38]	22 [14.10]
N	42	36	78	42	36	78	156

Figures given in brackets indicate percentage.

Most of the respondents i.e. 84.90 per cent said that vaccination and immunization camps are being organized. Such special devices have been reported to be significantly higher in Uttar Pradesh as compared to Uttaranchal (Table 12).

Though, Panchayatiraj Institutions have been strengthened to function as important instrument for distribution of contraceptives at community level, surprisingly no respondent accepted that there is any system of contraceptive distribution at Panchayat level (Table 13).

Table 13
Existence of System of Contraceptive Distribution at Panchayats

	Uttar Pradesh			*Uttaranchal*			*Total*
	Officials	*Non-officials*	*Sub-total*	*Officials*	*Non-officials*	*Sub-Total*	
Yes	-	—	-	-	-	-	-
No	42 [100.00]	36 [100.00]	78 [100.00]	42 [100.00]	36 [100.00]	78 [100.00]	156 [100.00]
Cannot say	-	-	-	-	-	-	-
N	42	36	78	42	36	78	156

Figures given in brackets indicate percentage.

Only 13 per cent respondents admitted that there is in place system for health counseling and education in the surveyed areas. It was reported comparatively higher in Uttaranchal than in Uttar Pradesh (Table 14).

Table 14
System for Health Counseling and Education

	Uttar Pradesh			*Uttaranchal*			*Total*
	Officials	*Non-officials*	*Sub-total*	*Officials*	*Non-officials*	*Sub-Total*	
Yes	8 [19.05]	-	8 [12.26]	12 [28.57]	-	12 [15.38]	20 [12.82]
No	34 [80.95]	30 [83.33]	64 [82.05]	30 [71.14]	23 [63.89]	53 [67.95]	117 [75.00]
Cannot say	-	6 [16.67]	6 [7.69]	-	13 [36.11]	13 [16.67]	19 [12.18]
N	42	36	78	42	36	78	156

Figures given in brackets indicate percentage.

More than half of the respondents said the NGO's are functioning for health services delivery. It was found more pronouncing in Uttaranchal as compared to Uttar Pradesh. (Table 15).

Table 15
Working of NGO for Health Service Delivery

	Uttar Pradesh			*Uttaranchal*			*Total*
	Officials	*Non-officials*	*Sub-total*	*Officials*	*Non-officials*	*Sub-Total*	
Yes	15 [35.71]	6 [16.67]	21 [26.92]	36 [85.71]	28 [77.78]	64 [82.05]	85 [54.49]
No	27 [64.29]	30 [83.33]	57 [73.08]	6 [14.29]	8 [22.22]	14 [17.95]	71 [45.51]
N	42	36	78	42	36	78	156

Figures given in brackets indicate percentage.

Table 16
Main Communicable Diseases

	Uttar Pradesh			*Uttaranchal*			*Total*
	Officials	*Non-officials*	*Sub-total*	*Officials*	*Non-officials*	*Sub-Total*	
HIV/AIDS/STD	6 [14.29]	-	6 [7.69]	3 [7.14]	5 [13.89]	8 [10.26]	14 [8.97]
TB	5 [11.90]	10 [27.78]	15 [19.23]	5 [11.90]	4 [11.11]	9 [11.54]	24 [15.38]
Cholera	12 [28.57]	32 [88.89]	44 [56.41]	6 [14.29]	6 [16.67]	12 [15.38]	56 [35.90]
Jaundice	17 [40.48]	21 [58.33]	38 [48.72]	21 [50.00]	8 [22.22]	29 [37.18]	67 [42.95]
Meningitis	5 [11.90]	3 [8.33]	8 [10.26]	12 [28.57]	6 [16.67]	18 [23.08]	26 [16.67]
Malaria	31 [73.81]	7 [19.44]	38 [48.72]	9 [21.43]	13 [36.11]	22 [28.21]	60 [38.46]
Hepatitis	-	-	-	2 [4.76]	4 [11.11]	6 [7.69]	6 [3.85]
Dengue	16 [38.10]	19 [52.78]	35 [44.87]	8 [19.05]	15 [41.67]	23 [29.49]	58 [37.18]
Others	42 [100.00]	36 [100.00]	78 [100.00]	35 [83.33]	34 [94.44]	69 [88.46]	147 [94.23]
N	42	36	78	42	36	78	156

Figures given in brackets indicate percentage.

The main communicable diseases occurring inthe area are shown in Table 16. Malaria, Dengue, Jaundice, Cholera and Meningitis are the main communicable diseases which are mainly water borne diseases and due to poor sanitary conditions. Their prevalence is found to be higher in Uttar Pradesh as compared to Uttaranchal.

The prevalence of non-communicable diseases are shown in Table 17. Drug abuse, cardio vascular disease and respiratory diseases are more common in the surveyed areas. These are more prevalent in Uttaranchal as compared to Uttar Pradesh.

Table 17
What are the other major Non-Communicable Diseases in your area

	Uttar Pradesh			*Uttaranchal*			*Total*
	Officials	*Non-officials*	*Sub-total*	*Officials*	*Non-officials*	*Sub-Total*	
Heart stroke	30	24	54	36	30	66	120
	[71.43]	[66.67]	[69.23]	[85.71]	[83.33]	[84.62]	[76.92]
Respiratory	12	5	17	21	24	45	62
	[28.57]	[13.89]	[21.79]	[50.00]	[66.67]	[57.69]	[39 74]
Diabetes	42	13	55	29	31	60	115
	[100.00]	[36.11]	[70.51]	[69.05]	[86.11]	[76.92]	[73.72]
Injuries	19	12	31	40	36	76	107
	[45.24]	[33.33]	[39.74]	[95.24]	[100.00]	[97.44]	[68.59]
Drug abuse	12	26	38	42	36	78	116
	[28.57]	[72.22]	[48.72]	[100.00]	[100.00]	[100.00]	[74.36]
Mental	8	15	23	10	9	19	42
	[19.05]	[41.67]	[29.49]	[23.81]	[25.00]	[24.36]	[26.92]
Others	42	30	72	40	30	70	142
	[100.00]	[83.33]	[92.31]	[95.24]	[83.33]	[89.74]	[9.03]
N	42	36	78	42	36	78	156

Figures given in brackets indicate percentage

The main factors contributinng to the spread of communicable diseases were reported mosquito breeding (56.41 per cent), poor quality of water (40.38 per cent), poor health education (45.51 per cent) and poor service of preventive medical care (42.31 per cent). The poor quality of water and mosquito breeding has been reported significantly higher in Uttar Pradesh as compared to Uttaranchal (Table 18).

Table 18
Main Factors of Communicable Diseases

	Uttar Pradesh			Uttaranchal			Total
	Officials	Non-officials	Sub-total	Officials	Non-officials	Sub-Total	
Poor quality of water	21 [50.00]	31 [86.11]	52 [66.67]	3 [7.14]	8 [22.22]	11 [14.10]	63 [40.38]
Poor health education	12 [28.57]	20 [55.56]	32 [41.03]	15 [35.71]	24 [66.67]	39 [50.00]	71 [45.51]
Mosquito breeding	40 [95.24]	36 [100.00]	76 [97.44]	7 [16.67]	5 [13.89]	12 [15.38]	88 [56.41]
Poor service of preventive medicine care	5 [11.90]	29 [80.56]	34 [43.59]	2 [4.76]	30 [83.33]	32 [41.03]	66 [42.31]
Unhealthy climate	3 [7.14]	4 [11.11]	7 [8.97]	-	-	-	7 [4.49]
Others	36 [85.71]	28 [77.78]	64 [82.05]	40 [95.24]	30 [83.33]	70 [89.74]	134 [85.90]
N	42	36	78	42	36	78	156

Figures given in brackets indicate percentage.

The main factors of poor state of health are shown in Table 19. Poor quality of health infrastructure, low community participation, poor delivery of health services and non-involvement of community based organizations in delivery of health services etc. were reported some of the main factors responsible for poor state of health.

The satisfaction regarding health services is shown in Table 20. Immunization, vaccination, RCH, MCH, health education, health counseling, home visit of health workers, and delivery of health care services etc. are reported to be quite satisfactory, however, child care services, functioning of hospitals and distribution of contraceptives have been found to be poor in the surveyed areas.

Overall, the analysis suggests that sanitary conditions have to be improved and effective functioning of government run health institutions/centres should be ensured in order to improve the health status of women and children. Moreover, community based organizations need orientation, sensitization and strengthening for taking active role in delivery of health services.

Table 19
Factors Responsible for Poor State of Health

	Uttar Pradesh			*Uttaranchal*			*Total*
	Officials	*Non-officials*	*Sub-total*	*Officials*	*Non-officials*	*Sub-Total*	
Poor delivery of health services	8 [19.05]	20 [55.56]	28 [35.90]	12 [28.57]	15 [41.67]	27 [34.62]	55 [35.26]
Poor educational standard	-	18 [50.00]	18 [23.08]	9 [21.43]	12 [33.33]	21 [26.92]	39 [25.00]
Poor quality of health services	2 [4.76]	15 [41.67]	17 [21.79]	8 [19.05]	21 [58.33]	29 [37.18]	46 [29.49]
Low community participation	15 [35.71]	10 [27.78]	25 [32.05]	18 [42.86]	30 [83.33]	48 [61.54]	73 [46.79]
Poor quality of health infrastructure	14 [33.33]	31 [86.11]	45 [57.69]	4 [9.52]	29 [80.56]	33 [42.31]	77 [49.36]
Non-involvement of CBOs, NGOs	15 [28.57]	30 [83.33]	42 [53.85]	3 [7.14]	10 [27.78]	13 [16.67]	55 [35.26]
Poor marketing and promotion of health care services	6 [14.29]	12 [33.33]	18 [23.08]	9 [21.43]	15 [41.69]	24 [30.77]	42 [26.92]
Others	26 [61.90]	30 [83.33]	56 [71.79]	28 [66.67]	31 [86.11]	59 [75.64]	115 [73.72]
N	42	36	78	42	36	78	156

Figures given in brackets indicate percentage.

Table 20
Satisfaction from Health Services

	Uttar Pradesh				*Uttaranchal*			
	Excellent	*Good*	*Poor*	*N*	*Excellent*	*Good*	*Poor*	*N*
Immunization	21 [28.92]	52 [66.66]	5 [6.41]	78	60 [76.92]	12 [15.38]	6 [7.69]	78
Vaccination	20 [25.64]	50 [64.10]	8 [10.25]	78	42 [53.84]	21 [28.92]	15 [19.23]	78
MCH	9 [11.53]	39 [50.00]	30 [38.46]	78	15 [19.23]	35 [44.87]	28 [35.89]	78
RCH	15 [19.23]	48 [61.53]	15 [19.23]	78	18 [23.07]	30 [38.46]	30 [38.46]	78
Health education	17 [21.79]	25 [32.05]	36 [46.15]	78	15 [19.23]	21 [28.92]	42 [53.84]	78
Health counselling	-	5 [6.41]	73 [93.58]	78	-	20 [25.64]	58 [74.35]	78
Distribution of contraceptives	28 [35.89]	29 [37.17]	21 [28.92]	78	25 [32.05]	45 [57.69]	8 [10.25]	78
Home visit of visitors	5 [6.41]	15 [19.23]	58 [74.35]	78	30 [38.46]	15 [19.23]	33 [42.30]	78
Functioning of Govt. run hospitals	30 [38.46]	34 [43.58]	14 [17.94]	78	34 [45.38]	20 [25.64]	24 [30.76]	78
Delivery of health care services	22 [28.20]	37 [47.43]	19 [24.35]	78	28 [35.89]	20 [25.64]	30 [38.48]	78
Child care services	10 [12.82]	42 [53.84]	26 [33.33]	78	20 [25.64]	15 [19.23]	43 [55.12]	78
Others	5 [6.41]	35 [44.87]	38 [48.71]	78	15 [19.23]	40 [51.28]	23 [29.48]	78

Figures given in brackets indicate percentage.

7

OBSERVATIONS AND POLICY RECOMMENDATIONS

It has been recognized that good health is definitely an important contributor to productivity and economic growth. In India, health assumes greater significance; however, Indian health scenario presents greater challenges. The low base of health indicators combined with overwhelming burden of available morbidity and mortality accounted for pre transition diseases make itquite impossible dramatic improvements in the health status in a relatively short time span. This calls for enhanced public investment, accompanied by wide ranging reforms at every level which can be achieved only with strong political will and commitment. Restructuring of the public health systems of the states is called for integrating preventive, promotive and curative services, decentralizing authority and providing health services to poor. Public private partnership is felt necessary in order to reduce the burden of health expenditure on public exchequer and to promote community based strategies, including comprehensive health education, counseling and providing RCH services. In order to reduce the burden of communicable and non-communicable diseases, efforts are needed to change the life style and promote AYUSH. The study attempts to examine the status of health care services for women and children in U.P. and Uttaranchal and to suggest measures for improving their health status.

OBSERVATIONS

There are very large disparities across different states and regions of India in terms of their performance on the Millennium Development indicators. The inter and intra state disparities have important implications for targeting of interventions and resources to the lagging states and regions.

- Millennium Development indicators have high levels of geographic concentration in India. One fifth of the villages and districts account for about one half of all the infant deaths and underweight children in the country.
- Gender disparity in health indicators is found to be high. It is estimated that overall child mortality in the country would drop by 20 per cent if girls had the same mortality rate as boys between the ages of 1 month and 5 years. Gender disparities in health and schooling outcomes are largely caused by parental discrimination against the girl child. Public Policies that increase the parental incentive to invest in girls, such as female scholarships or health care subsidies for girls, are likely to work well in narrowing the gender gap.
- A reduction in the proportion of underweight children is strongly associated with a reduction of child mortality. It is expected that interventions that reduce maternal mortality, such as vaccination against tetanus, immunization, expansion of antenatal care coverage and increase in the ratio of professionally attended deliveries will bring large reductions in infant mortality.
- Bihar, Uttar Pradesh, Madhya Pradesh, Orissa and Rajasthan account for a disproportionably large share of the country's population.
- A package of home based neonatal services is unlikely to reduce neonatal mortality ratio if health workers are not sufficiency motivated to reach out the community and deliver the package of services to the poor and vulnerable.

- There has been paradigm shifts in governance of health programmes in India. RCH is the main sexual health needs of women and adolescent girls. The recently launched National Rural Health Mission also highlights the role of country in providing health care services as well as improving reproductive health of women. As the country undergoes demographic and epidemiological transition, it is likely that longer investments in health will be needed even to maintain the current health status.
- The housing conditions, living conditions, as well as background of women have direct and indirect bearing on health status; however, their access to health care services and their health seeking behaviour vary from region to region and even community to community.
- Though, majority of the women are aware regarding health services as well the importance of contraceptives, immunization, vaccination, pre and post-natal care and institutional delivery of pregnancy, however, overall situation which emerges from the analysis of survey data demonstrates that a large number of women are being deprived of such services and living in risks. The availability of the RCH services also could not be ensured to the masses due to socio-cultural and geographical factors.
- The marriage patterns simply show that child marriage is still prevalent in northern states. A large number of marriages take place in adolescent age. Moreover, the proportion of marriages in adolescence age among girls is higher than their made counterparts.
- Only two-fifth women said that health workers visit their homes for antenatal checkup. About 60 per cent deliveries take place at home, without proper medical assistance which show vulnerability of pregnant mothers to complications and diseases.
- Only one-third women accepted that they used contraceptives for birth control and 28 per cent of them are still using them. A large number of them are still using them. A large number of respondents face problems in contraceptives use.

- The girls are discriminated against boys in providing vaccination and immunization. Moreover, daughter disadvantages are reflected in terms of sex determination of child in womb, nutrition, health checkup, medical treatment, schooling and marriage. Girls are married off early as compared to boys due to economic hardship, prevailing cultural traditions, and avoidance of dowry as well.
- The sanitation and scavenging conditions in the surveyed areas have been found poor. The existence of drainage system was reported by 20 per cent respondents only. Its absence causes waterborne disease.
- The communicable diseases, mainly Jaundice, malaria, dengue, cholera, and TB create burden on health in the surveyed areas while cardio-vascular, diabetes, injuries, drug abuse, cancer etc. are the main factors of communicable diseases end are related with poor quality of water, poor health education, mosquito breeding and poor access to health care services.
- Social marketing of health programmes especially for creating awareness and sensitizing community, government officials, non-officials, as well as community based organizations is called for. This approach may be highly useful in HIV/AIDS, sexual and reproductive health and adoption of indigenous systems of medicines.

RECOMMENDATIONS

Central Government

- There is a need to hold government accountable for enforcing the legal age of marriage for both boys and girls. The Child Marriage Prevention Act should be effectively enforced to prevent early marriages.
- More research is needed to understand how the situation and needs of married adolescents differ from those of married adults and unmarried adolescents.

- Special programmes may be taken in areas where IMR and child mortality are high to provide an integrated packages of services for improving the capacity of the system to manage common childhood concerns at field level.
- Adolescent girls need specific policies to address specified sectors like education, health, family welfare, nutrition, HIV/AIDS, sports, etc. An integrated and holistic development programmes for empowerment of adolescent girls are needed. Adolescents in different circumstances like adolescent with disabilities learning disorders, adolescent sex workers, children of sex workers and street children need more visibility and space in policies.
- Effective and efficient administration of Kishori Shakti Yojana, Balika Samridhi Yojana, Kasturba Gandhi Balika Shiksha Scheme and other such schemes oriented for empowerment of adolescent girls should be ensured and the coverage of such schemes be extended.
- Educational, nutritional, health, livelihood and recreational programmes need to be designed keeping in view of the socio-cultural expectations and economic pressures on adolescent girls.
- Reproductive and sexual health programmes are to be designed keeping in view the rights to health care services, right to information about prevention, reproduction, transmission of diseases, right to healthy life, nutrition, education, creation and freedom from violence and abuse. More emphasis is required for counselling, sensitization, education, and improving the health care services to meet the emerging needs of reproductive and sexual health of the adolescent girls.
- In order to reduce malnutrition, ICDS activities need to be refocussed on the most important determinants of malnutrition. Programmatically, this means emphasizing disease control and prevention activities, education to improve domestic child care, and feeding practices, and micronutrient supplementation. Greater convergence with

the health sector and in particular the RCH programme would help in this regard.

- ICDS activities need to be better targeted towards the most vulnerable age groups, while funds and new projects need to be redirected towards the states and districts with the highest degree of malnutrition.
- The supplementary feeding activities under ICDS programme need to be better targeted towards those who need it most, and growth monitoring activities needed to be performed with greater regularity, with more emphasis on understanding of parents that how health and nutritional status of their children may be improved.
- Monitoring and evaluation activities under ICDS, RCH and other health care programmes need strengthening through collection of timely relevant, accessible, high quality data and the performance should be measured on regular basis.
- States must be provided earmarked funding under health sector allocation in Plan proposals for primary health care services.

State Governments

- The mindset of administrators, policymakers, political leaders and service providers towards adolescent girls need to be changed and they should recognize that the needs and desires of adolescent girls are different from the needs and desires of adolescent boys.
- Health and nutrition education is very important for adolescent girls to create awareness regarding sexual and reproductive health as well as to help parents in understanding the importance of marriage and child bearing at matured age.
- Carrier and vocational guidance to the adolescent girls are important instruments for educational and economic empowerment of women.

- There is a need to improve content and quality of ongoing family welfare services, evolve appropriate indicators for monitoring quality of services and coverage levels.
- Services are needed that reach out beyond the clinics to enable young women to seek prenatal visits and adequate obstetric care and to obtain counseling or services relating to coercion and violence and STI symptoms.
- More research is needed on how the situation and needs of married adolescent girls differ from those of their married male counterparts and unmarried adolescent girls.
- Better understanding of the causes of the sexual and reproductive health needs of married adolescent, girls which remain unmet, why informed choice continues to elude them and how services should be structured to overcome the social, cultural and economic constraints that they face has to be understood in right perspective.
- All existing primary health care infrastructure be strengthened while adequate supplies of drugs and kits be ensured for effective and efficient delivery of RCH services. The gaps in required and existing health centres may be bridged through public private partnership and launching of mobile health clinics.
- Access to primary health care can be improved by establishing required primary health centres in areas inhabited by vulnerable/tribal population groups or in areas which have poor demographic indices.
- The primary health centres (PHCs) should function as curative care centres and also provide preventive and promotive health care and family welfare services, while CHC's should provide backup curative, referral and patient facilities.
- Availability of medical and paramedical man power should be improved through contractual appointment of health professionals.

- Sub centres may be strengthened in terms of improved facilities and infrastructure to provide services under RCH programme.
- There is urgent need for making the health care institutions at district level to be self sustainable so that these can function in a financially independent way to provide quality health care facilities.
- Suitable programmes under Continuing Medical Education (CME) should be planned involving community based organizations (NGOs, youth clubs, SHGs, Mahila Swasthya Sanghs, etc.). Village council and Panchayats may be motivated and strengthened to pay a critical role in medical education.
- Tele-health services may be strengthened by opening more information kiosks, connecting health centres on line, involving community based organization, particularly NGOs and district level Panchayats and urban local bodies.
- There is need to open new schools and institutions of public health sothat more public health professionals could be trained. The discipline of public health should also encompass disciplines like AYUSH, MCH, health administration, IEC, etc.
- Department of Community Medicine or Preventive and Social Medicine be strengthened and their branches be opened at different places to provide health education and community medicines.
- Inter sectoral coordinating mechanism on a strategy basis may be ensured for convergence of health services, availability of safe drinking water, sanitation, child development, nutrition etc. Regular analysis of various public policies and practices of various departments such as Environment, Urban Development, Rural Development, Health Education, Family welfare etc. must be considered essential pre-requisite for a meaningful inter-ministerial coordination.

- Primary health care may also be strengthened through efforts of diverse health providers by (1) accrediting private medical practitioners and assigning them to definite beneficiary groups to provide primary health and family welfare services especially in rural areas, (2) revival of the system of licensed medical practitioners who after certification from the Indian Medical Association could provide specified clinical services; (3) involvement of the non-medical fraternity in counseling and advocacy to promote RCH services.
- Public Private Partnership in the form of collaboration with NGOs and private sectors may be further strengthened and promoted. Its main areas may include management of information system, education, and communication, promotion of referral services transportation of patients to and from remote and inaccessible areas, provision of RCH care to their employers, creation of network of health centres, etc.
- Training to health personnel such as ASHA workers, Aganwadi workers, Nurses, Dais, Registered Medical Practitioners, representatives of NGOs and other community based organizations may be imparted to promote community participation in RCH services and improving the delivery of health care services.
- Special arrangements may be made to improve birth and death registration to get reliable state level estimates. This may be ensured through enhancing the role of NGOs SHGs, Panchayats, Mahila Swasthya Sanghs and urban local bodies.
- There is a need to improve content and quality of on going family planning services and evolve appropriate indicators for monitoring quality of services as well as its coverage levels.

OTHER LEVELS

- A massive awareness campaign involving the community, religious leaders and opinion makers at all levels is necessary to counter demographic imbalances along with effective policies and programmes in favour of girl child.

- A completely new strategy based on a holistic approach of awareness, incentives, education, nutrition and enforcement need to be worked out to protect the rights of the girl children. Women should have access o comprehensive, affordable and quality health care, which should gò beyond the reproductive health to take into account their vulnerability to various endemic, infections and communicable diseases. The social and health consequences of HIV/AIDS and sexually transmitted diseases also needed to be tackled from a gender perspective.
- Community participation should be promoted by encouraging and organizing orientation and training programmes for members of Mahila Swasthya Sanghs, SHGs, NGOs, Panchayats, local bodies, youth clubs, etc. These community based organizations may be engaged in RCH services as well as monitoring other health care services.
- Special programmes may be launched in areas where IMR and child mortality rates are high to provide an integrated packages of services for improving the capacity of the system to manage common childhood conditions.
- A mass awareness compaign for malaria, tuberculosis, HIV/AIDS, cancer, etc. should be held at fairs, and haats in rural areas to increased interaction of health workers with local population.
- There is a strong need of local IEC efforts, effective community utilization and social marketing of health programmes, services including distribution of contraceptives.
- Documentation of folk claims related to health, ecology and socio-cultural system could provide the model for appropriate health and sanitary practices in a given ecosystem. Identification of indigenous herbs for medical

use, their preservation and documentation and ethno botanical and ethno zoological museums for collection preservation and display of medicinal herbs may be developed in order to promote Ayurvedic and Unani treatment for diseases.

- Development and promotion of horticulture, poultry and fisheries may enhance quality intake for improving nutritional status of mothers and children. The quality food and nutritional diet intake may be promoted through effective communication strategies on health education and health care in consonance with socio-cultural characteristics of ethnic population.
- Marriage cum pregnancy counseling may be promoted by improving community participation, integrated schemes of child development, immunization and nutrition.
- Malnutrition among children may be checked through improved nutritional status of pregnant and lactating mothers, and also through health counseling for enhancing good quality and nutritional intake during pregnancy.
- Prenatal and postnatal checkup may be ensured by promoting public private partnership and mobilizing community.
- Antenatal checkup may be improved through concerted efforts of government and non-government agencies by launching special drives for health, nutrition and education.
- Imparting training to health personnel, strengthening health centres in terms of improved health facilities, hiring services of qualified health professionals and mobilizing pregnant mothers for institutional delivery with professional assistance may be ensured to reduce the risks of maternal health.
- Breast feeding may be promoted through imparting health and nutritional education and providing orientation to community leaders and community based organizations.

Integration of other development programmes with health programmes and also promoting nutritional and health status of pregnant and lactating mothers is required.

- Lactating mothers may be educated and counselled for vaccination while they may be advised to take proper treatment of diagnosed diarrhoea cases of their children.

REFERENCES

Ali, A. (1992), "Nutrition" IN: *State of India's Health* by A. Mukhopoadhyaya, VHAI, Delhi.

Alland, A. (1966), "Medical Anthropology and the Study of Biological and Cultural Adaptations", *American Anthropologists,* 68 (1).

Banerjee, D. (1982), "*Poverty Class and Health Culture in India*", Praimi Prakashan, New Delhi.

Bhasin, V. (1990), *Habitat, Habitation and Health in the Himalayas: A Comparative Study of the People of Sikkim and the Gaddis of Himachal Pradesh,* Kamal Raj Enterprises, Delhi.

Bhattacharya (1995), "Folk Medicinal Claims for the Treatment of Venereal Disease from Patalkot, Valley of Chchindwara Distt." *South Asian Anthropologist,* Vol. 1 (6).

Bott, Sarah and Jejeebhoy S.J. *Adolescents Sexual and Reproductive Health in South Asia: An Overview of Findings from the 2000 Mumbai Conference,* UNDP India.

Candila, W. (1953), "Applied Anthropology in Medicine", IN: *Anthropology Today,* (Ed.) A.L. Kapoor, University of Chicago Press.

Carstrairs, G.M. (1955), "Medicine and Faith in Rural Rajasthan" IN: Health, Culture and Community, (Ed.) Benjamin D. Paul, Russel Sage Foundation, New York.

Chakravarthy, M. & Singhrol, C.S. (1989), "Socio-Cultural and Environmental Aspects of Health and Nutrition", IN: *Anthropology: Some Socio-Demographic and Nutritional Aspects Of Health,* A.N. Sharma (Ed.), Northern Book Centre, Delhi.

Fabrega, Jr. (1972), "Medical Anthropology", IN: *Biennial Review of Anthropology,* Standford University Press, Standford.

Foster, G.M. And Anderson, G.A. (1978), *Medical Anthropology,* Jhon Willey & Sons, New York.

Ghosh, B.N. et. al. (2003), "Gender Differential in *Socio-Cultural Political*" and Health Aspects in Rural West Bengal, India, IN: *Dimensions of Researches In Indian Anthropology,* (Ed.) Sahay and Singh, Serials Publications, Delhi.

Government of India, "National Population Policy 2000", Ministry of Health and Family Welfare, New Delhi.

Guja, C. et.al. (2001), "Medical Anthropology—Anthropological Medicine", *The Oriental Anthropologist,* Vol. (1), Jan.

Hasan, K.A. (1967), *Cultural Frontiers of Health in Village India,* Manakplas, Bombay.

Hughes, C. (1968), "Ethro-medicine", IN: *International Encyclopaedia of Social Sciences,* (Ed.) David Sills) Crowell Collier and MacMillan.

Jaggi, O.P. (1973), *Folk Medicine,* Atma Ram, New Delhi.

Joshi, P.C. & Mir, U.A. (2002), "Medical Anthropology & Traumatic Reactions", *The Eastern Anthropologist,* Vol. 55 (1), Jan.-March.

Kapoor, A.K. (1998), "Ecology, Demographic Profile and Socio-Economic Development of Tribe of Central Himalaya", IN: *Tribal Development*: Options, (Ed.) P.K. Samal, Gyanodaya Prakashan, Nainital.

Kapoor, A.K. (1998), The Anthropologist as A Bio-Social Hero: Health Medicine and Majic in A Schedules Tribes of Himalaya (M). Andhra University, Vishakhapattanam.

Khongsdier R. (2003), "Maternal Education in Relation" to the Indicators of Health and Development in North East India. IN: *Dimensions of Researches in Indian Anthropology,* (Ed.) Sahay and Singh, Serials Publications. Delhi.

Landey, D. (Ed.) (1977), "Culture, Disease and Healing": *Studies in Medical Anthropology,* McMillan Publications, New York.

Leiben, R.W. (1973), "Medical Anthropology", IN: *Handbook of Social and Cultural Anthropology,* (Ed.), J.J. Horigwan, McNalley College Publications, Co. Chicago.

Lewis, O. (1958), *Village Life in Northern India,* Random House, New York.

Marrio. H.M. (1955), "Western Medicine in a Village of Northern India", IN: Health Culture and Community, (Ed.) Benjamin D. Paul, Russel Sage Foundation, New York.

Mishra, Pramod (2004), Ecology, Culture and Health, Serials, Publications, Delhi.

Mishra, R. et. al. (2003), "India Health Report", OUP, Delhi.

Mitra, K. et. al. (1998), "Health Problems and Practices of Slum Women of Delhi", *South Asian Anthropologist*, Vol. 1 (19).

Mitra, K., (2003), "Gender, Development and Women Health in India", *Indian Journal of Social Development*, Vol. 3 (1), June.

Mohammad, N. et. al. (2003), "Convergence Approach for the Promotion of Reproductive and Child Health: Learning From Lodha Block Experience, "*Indian Journal of Social Development*", Vol. 3 (1).

Opler, M.E. (1963), "The Cultural Definition of Illness in Village India", *Human Organization*, 22.

Pachori, S. (1993), *Medical Geography of Malaria in M.P.*, Northern Book Centre, Delhi.

Pandey S.P. and Singh A.K.S "Theme Paper on Community Participation in RCH Services in India", Pandit Govind Ballabh Pant Institute of Studies in Rural Development, Lucknow, 11-12 February 2006.

Pandey, A. et al. (1998), *Infant and Child Mortality in India*, IIPS, Mumbai.

PFI Ensuring Quality of Care in Reproductive Health, Population Foundation of India, New Delhi, 2004.

Planning Commission, *Report of the Steering Committee on Family Welfare for Tenth Five Year Plan*, Govt. of India, September 2002.

Planning Commission, *Report of the Steering Committee on Health for Tenth Five Year Plan*, Govt. of India, September 2002.

Planning Commission, *Report of the Subgroup on Public Health*, Govt. of India, July 2001.

Planning Commission (2001), *Report of the Working Group on Adolescents for Tenth Five Year Plan*, Planning Commission, Govt. of India.

Planning Commission, (2001), *Report of the Working Group on Health Care for Women & Children for Tenth Plan*, Planning Commission, Govt. of India.

Planning Commission, (2001), *Report of the Working Group on Health Care Services for Tenth Five Year Plan*, Planning Commission, Govt. of India.

Prasad, R.R. & Kapoor, A.K. (1982), "Obstetrical Practices Among The Bhotia Tribes", *Vanjanjati*, 4.

Ramchandra, P. (2002), "Health Nutrition, Population Vision 2020", IN: *Indian Vision 2020*, Planning Commission, Govt. of India.

Ramchandran, S., (2003), "Women Status Effect on Family Size", IN: *Dimensions of Researches in Indian Anthropology*, (Ed.) Sahay and Singh, Serials Pubications, Delhi.

Ranjan, "Geetika, Role of Elites in the Development of the Bhoxa Tribes", *The Oriental Anthropologist, Vol. 2 (1)*, Jan., 2002.

Rizvi, S.N.H. (1998), "Practice of Native Medicine among the Jaunsari" IN: *Perspective in Tribal Development*, (Ed.) Saxena, H.S. et. al., Bharat Book Centre, Luckow.

Rizvi, S.N.H., (1986), "Health Practices of the Jaunsaris: A Socio-Cultural Analysis", IN: *Tribal Health: Socio-Cultural Dimensions*, (Ed.), B. Chaudhary, Inter-India Publication, Delhi.

Roney, J.G. (1959), Medical Anthropology: A Synthetic Discipline, *New Physician*, 8 (3).

Roy Burman, B.K., "Morbidity and Nutritional Status Of The Scheduled Tribes Of India", IN: *Tribal Health: Socio-Cultural Dimensions*, (Ed.), Chaudhary, B., Inter-India Pub. Delhi.

Sachchidananad, "Socio-Cultural Dimensions of Tribal Health" IN: *Tribal Health in Indian*, (Ed.), Basu, S., Manak Publications, Delhi.

Sahay, V.S. and Singh, P.K. (Ed.) (2003), *Dimensions of Researchers In Indian Anthropology*, Serials Publications, Delhi.

Samal, P.K. (1998), *Tribal Development: Options*, Gyanodaya Prakashan, Nainital.

Sankhyana, A.R. (1998), "Trends of Demographic Change in the Tharu" IN: *Perspective in Tribal Development*, (Ed.) Saxena, H.S. et. al., Bharat Book Centre, Luckow.

Sarala Gopalan & Mira Shiva (Ed). (2000), *National Profile in Women, Health and Development*, Voluntary Health Association of India and World Health Organization, Delhi.

Scotch, N. (1963), "Medical Anthropology", *Biennial Review of Anthropology,* Standford Ur iversity Press, Standford.

Singh S.K. and Singh A.K. Reproductive Child Health in North East Region, Serials Publications, New Delhi 2006.

Singh, A.K. (1996), *Tribes and Tribal Life* Vol. I, Sarup & Sons, New Delhi.

Singh, A.P., "Concept of Disease & Healing Among The Folk Cultures of Uttaranchal Himalaya," *The Oriental Anthropologist, Vol. 2 (1), Jan., 2002.*

Singh, U.P. (2003), "Trends of Mortality Among Bhoxa Tribe of Uttaranchal," *The Oriental Anthropologist,* Vol. 3 (1), Jan.

Sunder, R. (1995), *Household Survey of Health Care Utilization and Expenditure,* NCAER, New Delhi.

VHAI Health and Development Challenges of Chhattishgarh, Jharkhand and Uttaranchal, *Voluntary Health Association of India,* New Delhi, 2002.

World Bank Attaining the Millennium Development Goals in India, Oxford University Press, New Delhi 2005.

INDEX